THERE SHOULD BE BLOOD

VOLUME 1

T A RICHARDSON

eBook ISBN: 978-1-965161-48-7

Paperback ISBN: 978-1-965161-49-4

Hardback ISBN: 978-1-965161-50-0

Dedication

For Eva, Lukas and Rory

Contents

Dedication i

About the Author iii

Introduction iv

Chapter 1 August 28, 2020 1

Chapter 2 August 29 & 30 6

Chapter 3 August 31 11

Chapter 4 The Next Week 15

Chapter 5 September 14 31

Chapter 6 September 18 45

Chapter 7 September 28 52

Chapter 8 October 2 61

Chapter 9 October & November 67

Chapter 10 Christmas 77

Chapter 11 Boxing Day 88

Chapter 12 January 2021 94

Chapter 13 A Year On 111

Acknowledgment 121

About the Author

T A Richardson is a storyteller, coach, and advocate for social enterprise who thrives on connecting with people and inspiring positive change. Born in Northamptonshire, UK, Tim moved to London with his teenage sweetheart at 22, embracing a dynamic life that eventually led him to Cambridge. Known for his warmth and humor, Tim's passion for storytelling shines in his writing and speaking engagements worldwide. When he's not crafting tales or coaching leaders, he spends his time, walking and watching live sports and spending time with his grandchildren.

Introduction

The year 2020 will be remembered by us all for the disruption, fear and life-changing impact caused by the coronavirus Covid-19. Nowhere on earth was exempt from its reach. As for me, Covid-19 was something of a parallel story.

Naturally, as for everyone, my life was turned on its head by the arrival of this virus from China with a name like a soft drink. It was simply impossible to ignore. It felt like there was nowhere you could go that was beyond its reach.

Then there was the potential of, well, dying from it. Discriminate it did not. Old, young, thin, large, western, eastern, fit, or couch potatoes all fell victim to it. All our lives were halted, put on hold, open then closed. Families didn't see each other for months on end. Lonely old people were more at risk than ever of being overlooked as hatches were battened down everywhere. Skies fell silent. Streets emptied. Cafes and bars simply put chairs on to tables and locked the doors.

This would be tough enough to live through. Then, on top of that, something equally unexpected arrives in your world, like an alien from outer space.

Life is like that.

One minute, you think you have it all sussed, and you have plans in place, holidays to book, decorating to do, shows to see, and the next moment, like an unexpected squall on a summer day, you are caught without a coat or umbrella on the side of hill miles from any shelter. These are the times when you simply must accept that you are going to get wet, dig deep, and grin through the discomfort.

Maybe…

I have been encouraged to share something of this moment, not out of an arrogant sense that I have some profound insight or wisdom, but simply because it is quite a tale of absurdities, of joy, of love, and of fear. I am acutely aware that, over these recent months, thousands of people have had far more devastating life stories to share that would be much more worthy of our focus.

Many have been told across various media, and our lives have been impacted by them. But so many have gone and will be untold because they happened to ordinary people in ordinary places quietly amidst the global noise. I like to think that they will not have gone unnoticed or been silent to the universe and to God.

Just as this little chapter in my life has not.

Chapter 1
August 28, 2020

In February, the world has been hijacked by an invisible enemy called Covid-19, which is spreading inexorably across the globe as if in some blockbuster disaster movie. We have emerged from enforced imprisonment, the real meaning of 'lockdown', you understand, into the sunny delights of August during which we can 'eat out to help out.' Joy knows no bounds! Little do I know I am about to encounter a second hidden disease, only this time one much closer to home.

So it is that, on a Friday afternoon, I visit my local small hospital for what I think is a relatively routine blood test.

Backtracking a few days, I had visited my doctor to see if a lump on my neck was something that should concern me. The lump had been there for a few weeks, and, like most men, I rather expected it to just go away like most things do. But it hadn't. So, having negotiated my way into the doctor's surgery via a secret back door – coronavirus measures meant that I could not enter through the front door (I wondered how it was any different, as I still got inside) – the doctor looked at the lump and proceeded to prod around my neck and armpits.

"You'll need a blood test," she said.

"Fair enough," I replied. And that's when the fun began.

To be accurate, it had probably started months, if not years, before as something was afoot and developing inside me that I was not aware of. Think *Alien*. And this thing was about to reveal itself.

The Friday test was at 12.30 pm. Everything was normal through that particular process. Then, I received a phone call from the surgery itself, at about 4 pm, informing me that I needed to go to Princess Alexandra Hospital in Harlow immediately.

"What!!?"

"Yes, your blood test has revealed you have very low haemoglobin levels, and you may need a blood transfusion right away."

"What!!? When you say low, what are we talking about?"

"75."

"OK, what's that out of? I am thinking if it's 100 then that seems pretty high to me – a solid pass – but if it's 1000 then I see your point."

"Normal levels are around 130-140."

"Oh. Not so strong then. And you mean immediately, like today, now?"

"Yep."

"OK then, can I have some written permission from you at the surgery that I can wave at them in the hospital that says I have come in search of blood?"

"Sure, come by and we will give you a letter." Blimey. This is a turn up, I thought.

Next, I call my wife Caroline, who happens to be 60 miles away at the café we own and run in St Neots. Not convenient! I tell her I will drive over to Harlow; it's about 15 miles from our home.

En route, I collect the letter, again via some secret process that involves me waving my hands in a kind of friendly manner outside the surgery's main door and being passed a letter back through the letterbox, a sort of reverse posting. How weird. But little do we know how weird things are going to get under Covid.

As I am in the village where my son Josh works in the local gastro pub, I figure I will call in to see him and advise him of the news. He promptly insists on accompanying me to the hospital, bless him.

We arrive at Accident & Emergency, which is where I have been told to go (I follow instructions, you see). This time, I can go in through the front door, but only on my own. My wife, who has arrived from St Neots, and Josh can only watch from outside as I am consumed by A&E.

I am a tad nervous, of course, as I have never had a blood transfusion before and, therefore, have no idea what is about to ensue. I approach the 'Permission to Enter' window and proudly produce the letter that I assume will explain everything. I subsequently discover that it simply says: 'Please let this 60-year-old male patient into A&E as he may need a blood transfusion.' Helpful?

"You don't look 60," the receptionist says, looking up from the desk.

Not the first words I expected her to utter, I confess, but flattering, nonetheless.

"Thanks."

"You should take a seat," she adds.

Do I look that sick then, I wonder, or is this standard practice for all 60-year-olds? Who knows? I sit down, careful to avoid the taped-off seats. And there I sit for some time. Quite a long while, actually, and as early evening turns to early night, the gathering of genuinely injured and sick people is joined by an exceedingly loud and very large guy who is clearly homeless (he has a huge suitcase with him) and probably drunk or high. You can imagine what follows – insults, protests, rants, extreme tutting from other attendees, security guards, and police. It did alleviate the boredom.

Once I was eventually invited in to see someone, my blood pressure and pulse proved I was generally OK, and I was asked a couple of profoundly hard questions.

"So, Mr Richardson, you seem to be chronically anaemic. Do you know why that is?"

You are joking, I thought. I decide not to answer in my usual facetious manner, as if I'd picked up some chronic anaemia tablets from the chemist and popped the lot.

"Nope, I don't," I replied.

"Are you bleeding a lot, say in your pee or poo?"

"Nope."

"Are you sure?"

Well, I think I would have noticed, and I can't say that I have noticed pools of blood behind me as I walk along. Basically, I seem to be pretty secure when it comes to retaining the whole blood thing, I feel, on balance.

It's late now and it turns out that they don't do walk-in blood transfusions after all. Who knew, eh? Mind you, I guess that's a good thing really as we would soon have the rich and famous dropping in for a top-up of elixir juice and Friday drunks demanding a transfusion of cheap red wine.

"Can you come back tomorrow morning?"

"Well, I guess so." If it's that serious it would seem bonkers not to.

"Good, come to the Ambulatory Care Department." Ah… that would be walk-in then, after all.

Chapter 2
August 29 & 30

It turns out that Ambulatory Care is code for waiting room, and being seen by another bunch of kind and well-meaning NHS nurses and doctors. Again, on my own, I am asked to take another blood test because clearly, the first one caused such a state of utter disbelief in the NHS team that they needed to corroborate that I could actually still be walking with a count of 75. I oblige, and once a long time has elapsed, I was invited back to see a doctor.

"Your haemoglobin levels are 75."

"Yep, I was told this yesterday." Should I officially be dead by now, I wonder?

"You're chronically anaemic." Yep, I was told that too.

"Are you bleeding from anywhere?"

This is clearly a standard NHS question, I surmise, and quite a good one if you think about it as if I was bleeding from anywhere, then it would be a clear sign that things are not as they should be, like in a Hollywood sci-fi contagion-type film.

"Nope. I have not seen any sign of this."

"Perhaps in your poo?"

"Nope."

"We had better check."

"How?"

Finger-up-the-bum time to see if there's black residue, as

apparently, blood in your poo is black, not red. Confused? Yes. All clear there.

"We will need to do some tests as there could be something else going on internally," the doctor informs me. "In the meantime, we will get some blood and give you a transfusion."

I have read up on anaemia and noted that the symptoms included breathlessness and fatigue. This explains why, for the previous several months, I have been getting increasingly tired walking my dog through the woods and up hills to our home. It also explains why I have become increasingly exhausted walking around the golf course and find pushing my trolley uphill virtually impossible. It is, therefore, plausible. But why this should hit me as a healthy 60-year-old with no history of such is a mystery.

I wait in a rather comfy chair, it should be noted, for ages. Fortunately, I have a good book, and there is tea nearby. A few puzzled nurses seem to be wondering why I am still hanging around in the room that I shall henceforth refer to as the 'receiving room' – where people sit and receive blood. All I am doing is reading and drinking tea. I am clearly not a homeless drunk, but I do attract a few strange looks and the occasional question.

"Are you waiting for test results?"

"Nope. Had those," I reply in as non-vampire tone as I can muster.

"I am waiting for blood! Apparently, I need some more."

"Oh, that's fine then."

The doctor, whose name I have been trying my hardest to deduce from various passing mutterings from him and nurses, returns and breaks the news.

"We haven't got any."

What, blood? This is a hospital, for goodness' sake.

"No," he explains, "What I mean is we need some rather special blood for you as you have some antibodies in your Type A+ and we need to make a good match. We can't just go putting any old blood in you."

"Well, that's thoughtful," I respond gratefully. He explains that if I came back tomorrow, they will have some and I can have the transfusion then.

"Oh, good," I say. Can't I just sit here and read my book and doze for the next 12 hours?

Caroline is summoned to collect me – minus my additional blood – whereupon I break the news that, as expected, I am so unique and special that they need a rare form of A+ only found on the plains of Siberia.

The following day, I am back in Ambulatory Care, expectantly seeking blood. Doctor What's-his-name (he hasn't been wearing a name badge) invites me to have another blood test just in case things have changed overnight. As if. I offer up my arm yet again and I am punctured accordingly. However, this time something is wrong. The nurse looks ponderously at my arm as if it is something from a *Shrek* movie or the like.

"I can't get any blood," she says.

"I know the feeling," I say, "I've been here three days waiting for some."

"No, your arm isn't yielding any. There should be blood coming into the syringe, but there isn't."

Clearly, they have finally discovered the problem that has been true all along. I appear to have been operating on considerably less blood than is ideal, and she has, by chance, just tapped into the part of me that is empty just now. Maybe we should try the other arm.

At this point, I mention that, as a 20-year-old, I once volunteered to give blood, only to find that I was totally useless at it. Not only was I a 'slow bleeder' (it's an official category of citizen), but also pathetically squeamish as I just about passed out having given one-quarter of a pint.

"Oh," she says, "That explains it."

She goes into the other arm with more success. My right arm is presumably more stocked with blood, which explains why I can write with it and do other normal functions of life, whereas my left arm might just wither before my eyes it seems.

I rejoice in the fact that I am stingy when parting with blood, although this will continue to be a problem I will discover over the coming months.

The blue, comfy chairs await me, and I pick one in the corner of the receiving room. Book and tea to hand, I settle down and then, wonder of wonders, there is blood. I am punctured again, only this time in my hand to receive the cannula and the special brew. I have no experience with this procedure, and I am a tad thrown when I am told it will take three hours.

"Wow, that's slow," I say.

"Well, we could do a fast pump operation, but that would

cause your veins to explode," the nurse explains.

"OK, let's not do that then."

I realise why the blue chairs are so unexpectedly comfortable as I am going to be sitting in one for three hours. Later, when I am officially done, I am ready to leave as the nameless doctor tells me to come back tomorrow for some more tests to see if it has made a difference. Deep joy.

Chapter 3
August 31

It is time for a further blood test. This time I am more forthcoming with my offering. It reveals that I am still performing terribly on the haemoglobin index, so I need another pint of blood.

"Gosh," I say.

As a non-medic, I am curious at this point as to how this all works. I wonder if I should ask the obvious question.

"Can I enquire as to where all this new blood is going? Have I been operating with something akin to a large airlock in my circulatory system such that there is room for an additional two pints, or am I going to slosh about as I walk along because I have 10 pints in me rather than the usual eight?"

The kindly doctor looks at me for a moment, clearly considering whether he should respond at all or treat me like the numpty I clearly am. He decides that it would be cruel to keep me guessing.

"Clever thing, your body," he responds. "As it magically absorbs the blood and circulates the oxygen around your body. Your body, on the other hand, has not been doing that so well of late, which is why you are anaemic. We need to find out what is causing this anaemia. We should schedule a lymph node biopsy and a bone marrow biopsy. I have arranged for the haematology specialist to see you once you are done with the transfusion."

"Oh," I say, now in a state of increasing anxiety. Biopsy is one of those words hardly ever used in normal conversation by normal people. It is on the same level as phrases like 'nuclear blast' and 'extreme frostbite.'

The new blood drips hypnotically into me. I don't feel any different. Did I expect to?

I meet the haematology doctor in a discreet room. She has a wonderfully exotic accent that I spend the entire time trying to place. Kind of Italian, I think, but not purely so. This is a distraction from the important matters. There is clearly something up with my blood.

"What, even the new stuff," I protest. "You've only just given it to me."

"No, the old stuff, and there is clearly something going on internally that we need to investigate," she explains. "Biopsies, to be accompanied by a gentle endoscopy."

That all sounds such fun. "When are we talking about?"

At this point, I am mulling over whether to tell them that we are due to move house in 10 days' time to Huntingdon, which is 50 miles away, and that popping in for the occasional endoscopy was not in the plan. I decide not to.

"Immediately," the doctor says.

"What, like today?"

"No, maybe tomorrow or in the next few days."

"Ah, so this is urgent then."

"Yes," she adds and then, when I ask her what might be going on, she begins a rather long explanation that is essentially a stream of consciousness comprising her entire PhD thesis without repetition, deviation, or hesitation. She could be on the radio. I still cannot place her accent, which bothers me. Bothering me in equal measure is the dawning that I have something bad. Probably dreadful. Once she pauses for air, I seize the moment.

"Where is your accent from? Are you Italian?"

She clearly wasn't expecting that as the first question from the dying patient. I guess normal people ask about prognosis, which would make sense. I will come to that in a moment.

She explains that she comes from Serbia via Greece and now the UK. Different. My curiosity satiated; I try to summarise what I think she has told me. Basically, they are guessing that I have some form of lymph-related disease.

"Could be," she confirms.

"Lymphoma possibly." I gulp.

They take some more blood to test if the new stuff has found its way to my arm. Most likely, I reckon, as it was put into my hand. I head out, this time to the ear, nose and throat clinic because I was invited to go there by the NHS automated appointment arranging service. A letter had arrived saying that an appointment had been set up for me, and I dutifully wander over for my late afternoon appointment. This is to check what the lumps might be, I assume.

Now don't get me wrong, I am increasingly impressed by the NHS and how they are trying to use technology to improve things. This time, however, something had gone wrong. I discover that they were not expecting me in person, and it seems I should have phoned in and done this virtually.

My simple mind wonders how you can investigate anything on a body 'virtually,' especially down my throat. Should I wedge my cell phone down there with the flashlight on? But, as I am to find out over the coming months, anything is possible. A rather rushed and self-confident doctor graciously agrees to see me in person rather than make me stand outside and dial in to comply with the invitation. He checks down my throat and feels the lumps. No idea. Maybe come back in a couple of weeks once you have had the tests, he advises. This never happens.

Chapter 4
The Next Week

I judiciously avoid checking Google to see what lymphoma looks like, how it manifests itself, how it is treated, and what my chances of survival are. Wise, I think. Caroline, I suspect, does, though. Unwise. These things are written with the best intentions, of course, but when you do not have an informed, actual human to discuss these with, then every symptom is real, and every consequence is inevitable.

Nonetheless, the days following the Serbian doctor's rather matter-of-fact analysis based on some early blood tests and the fact that I was not bleeding externally are not easy. I meet with friends and explain some of the points, but as we are moving house soon, we have plenty to occupy us.

The blood test results come back and say that my haemoglobin levels are up a smidgeon to 78. I am still in D-minus grade territory, though. The hospital called and invited me to come for a lymph node biopsy on September 10 and with a CAT scan a day later. I do check on Google about CAT scans because I have a pathological fear of being put head-first into one of those tube things and being told to lie perfectly still for ages. Turns out, that's an MRI scanner and what I am to undergo is not the same. No tube involved. Phew! Little do I know…

It is the morning of September 10, and we are panicking because the need to put even more things into boxes never ends. The removal company has given us 140 boxes! If you have ever moved house, you will recognize this phenomenon, but if you have never actually seen 140 flat-packed cardboard boxes, like us, you will be in for a surprise. It is akin to bringing 50 fence panels into your house and being told to carry on as if they were not there. I mean, who has room for 50 fence panels?

These flat packs were big enough in their flat form but then they must be filled. We have a lot of stuff. Books, CDs (yes, I still believe in owning something tangible with actual images and even printed words), more books, pictures, more books, and more pictures. Add to this the contents of my wife's glass art studio – comprising lots of pieces of glass and a kiln that weighs half a ton – and you can see why the removal company asked us to split the move into two halves.

The first half is today, the 10th. All our non-essential furniture and stuff is going to be put into storage for 10 days or so because, for our buyers, we generously agreed to move out of our house 10 days before moving into our new house, which is still not finished and signed off yet. The emptying begins, and I supervise a bit, and then my lift to the hospital arrives. We've agreed that Caroline will stay at home to at least apologise for the heavy kiln, then she can come and collect me once I am done. If only it was that straightforward.

The Department of Nuclear Medicine sounds pretty dramatic, doesn't it? For once, I am not heading to Ambulatory Care but to the nuclear bunker. I expect to descend several flights of stairs and pass through heavy metal doors in thick concrete walls, but I am disappointed when I find it is just across the corridor from Ambulatory Care. Clearly nobody here is concerned about possible radiation leaks. I am summoned for a CAT scan as someone thinks that it would make sense to do that and the biopsy on the same visit.

Well, it sort of makes sense, but I wasn't expecting it, so I am a little thrown.

And then, this CAT scanner operator (name not given) asks me to take off my top layers and receive a dye in my arm. Apparently, this then lights up offending nodes like the Blackpool Illuminations for the X-ray machine. Well, nobody told me about this.

Do I get a choice of colour, I wonder?

Nope.

The whole procedure is done with the pace of a Jamie Oliver recipe – bish-bash-bosh and I am done, it seems. I have been laid out and circumnavigated by a large shiny doughnut that has moved up and down my now illuminated body like a 3D printer. I am told that my now familiar doctor, whose name I think has been shortened to Alli, is in the next room and will be looking at the scan. Fair enough.

I wait for a very short while on a hospital bed fully clothed, which feels a tad odd, and then I am wheeled a few yards down the corridor into a small, dark room. I could have walked, of course, but hey. I am greeted by two petite women doctors of Asian origin (names given and instantly forgotten, I am ashamed to say) and a nurse who is West African and is, shall we say, not petite. These details are important because the room itself is not large and contains various torture devices masquerading as ultra-sound biopsy tools and monitors. These are on a large mobile stand that is plugged to the mains. There is also a table and some cupboards and some chairs, I think, although it's dark and difficult to see clearly. And into this comes a full-sized bed. It's going to get cosy in here. Then the fun starts.

I am presumably lying here like a chain of Christmas lights having been illuminated by the dye. There's a very professional welcome and invitation to remove my top layers, lie on my side and lift my arm above my head, revealing my armpit. At this point, I am beginning to suspect all is not as it should be as I was expecting the biopsy to be on the lump on my neck as previously advised.

Nope.

I am assured that it won't hurt as I will be anaesthetised, locally. They are going to locate a node to sample and then will pierce me with what looks like a kind of long thin screwdriver, the kind an electrician might have. Apparently, this will be inserted into my body and then will clip pieces of the lymph node off.

"You'll hear a click," I am told.

Ah, so a kind of click-and-collect, I ponder. I am not convinced.

The more experienced doctor proceeds to begin probing with the ultrasound scanner into my armpit. This is uncomfortable, by which I mean very uncomfortable. Then, I am invited to roll over on to my other side to see 'if there is a better one to sample.'

When I do this, it becomes apparent that the machinery is on the wrong side of the bed. The nurse moves the bed over a little which merely traps the medics and machinery in a much smaller space. The doctor reaches over me with the device to see if she can get a better image.

"This is a good one," she says to her colleague. "What do you think?"

What I hear is something along the lines of: "Wow, this is a whopper; we can get a good large sample from it. This guy is in a bad way. He could be gone by next week if we aren't quick."

I begin to catastrophise in my mind, and then my body does something very peculiar. I begin to shake.

At the same time, the large, cheerful nurse who is trapped at the base of the bed has moved me back to the original position, thereby freeing the doctors who ask me to turn over again and stick my arm above my head. I am not sure whether I should be on my front, back, or side at this point. My brain, on the other hand, has resolved that I should get the hell out of here immediately.

"Are you alright?" they ask.

"Not really," I say, not wishing to reveal the full extent of my increasing panic.

"Could I have some water?"

"Sure."

It doesn't pay to be truthful.

The prodding resumes as the doctor tries to locate the 'whopper' of a light bulb in my armpit. My primitive brain is now going into overdrive. Get out, it tells me. This is a dangerous place! You are going to die shortly, so you need to run away! My developed and mature 60-year-old brain tries to fight it. Don't be so daft. You look like an idiot behaving like this. Pull yourself together.

Fat chance.

If you have ever experienced a panic attack, then you will know something about what I am talking about. I have only ever experienced them in confined spaces like tube trains or lifts. The cheerful nurse asks me if I have experienced anything like this reaction before. My humour still works as I tell her that I have never had a lymph node ultrasound biopsy before, so I am trying to process the whole scenario for the very first time. I am embarrassed. Now my legs start shaking, and there is a weird sensation in them as if someone has poured a warm liquid sherbet into me.

"Someone did pour dye into me. Maybe it's that," I say.

"Could be," she replies. "Some people do get a reaction to the dye." Now they tell me.

The procedure continues. The two ultrasound doctors are gleeful as they have found the perfect offender to take a chunk out of. She goes for it, and I do indeed hear a couple of clicks amidst the now overwhelming noise in my head. This is a genuine fear, amygdala hijack. Fight or flight? I need to fly in a big way. I teach this stuff – emotional intelligence. Control your emotions maturely. Choose between stimulus and response. Simple, eh? Not.

Right now, adrenaline is being manufactured by my body on an industrial scale and being pumped around me with the force of a fire appliance. I have an impending sense that I might launch myself off the bed and simply smash my way out of the room like the incredible hulk. Fortunately, I don't.

They're done now. They have some good material to analyse. They will send this off to the lab and the results will be fed back in a few days. The nurse, I am told, will wheel me back into the ward where I can take my time to recover before heading home.

Can't these people see that I am a wreck just now? I return to the ward, still on the bed, now shaking and tingling all over. I must resemble a fish that has been caught and is thrashing around on the bank. I am alone and genuinely frightened.

The cheerful nurse takes my blood pressure and looks anxious. This does not help my mood. It is dropping.

"You need to calm yourself down and just relax," she instructs me.

Try telling a dying fish to 'just relax.' I hear the words she says, but my now completely irrational brain translates them into: 'Forget calming down; you need to escape these dementors – now!' I cannot, of course.

I tell her that I need to call my wife and ask her to come over. I try to explain what on earth is happening to me, although, I suspect, not very clearly. The nurse fetches me some diazepam – a half tablet – to try to relax my body. A different doctor appears and looks at me in disbelief. What on earth is going on with this bloke, he must have thought. He looks like a flailing fish.

He then asks me if this leg shaking thing is voluntary or involuntary.

"Do you think I want to be behaving like this," I say. "I cannot control this at all."

"Oh dear," he responds. "Let's give the diazepam a few minutes to work."

Caroline arrives after I have been lying on this recovery bed for 40 minutes or so, not recovering at all. My blood pressure is falling but has stabilised, it appears. The nurse is still not cheerful enough in my mind. I am given more diazepam. This is beginning to resemble a scene from an episode of *House* where they try to work out why I have reacted like this. And then things get even more weird. It is 5 pm and the nuclear unit is closing.

"You will have to go to A&E because you cannot stay here," I am told.

"Are you serious?" I ask.

"Yes."

"Your wife can wheel you in a chair round there. We cannot let you go home in this state."

I flail into a wheelchair, and we make the trip to A&E, arrive, and then attempt to explain why on earth I am here. I suspect I am put into the category of 'the uncontrolled drunk man who has fallen over and cut himself.'

We wheel over to a row of seats to wait. My legs are aching profoundly, and I can feel the adrenaline coursing around me as it consumes my glycogen at an alarming rate. I wonder if I am still lit up from the dye, flashing like a Belisha beacon in the corner of A&E. It would help if I was, as it would be evidence of the need for me to be here. As it is, I suspect I am something of a curiosity as I look normal, for a flailing fish in a wheelchair that is.

Eventually, after an eternity of waiting, I am ushered in to see someone. The explanation takes a while as the look of amazement increases on the face of the doctor.

"Is this involuntary shaking, then?" he asks.

Graciously, I responded by saying that I would not have chosen to shake for several hours and spend the day in the hospital. So yes, it is involuntary.

"Oh, that's very strange. Have you had these panic attacks before?"

It was starting to sound like a broken record.

"No," I insist.

"Well, we can give you some more calming drugs – this time, it's actually morphine."

Caroline and I settled into one of the A&E pens, shielded by a curtain from the rantings of an inebriated couple with, shall we say, a limited vocabulary of insults and protests about not being seen. Well, it is entertaining.

I am reminded of Robin Williams' portrayal of Patch Adams and the role humour and clowning around could have in a hospital A&E. My body is still not at ease with itself but, eventually, the medics agree that Caroline can head home, and they will admit me to a ward bed that night to ensure nothing more untoward is going on.

At around 3a.m., I am wheeled upstairs to a crowded ward, although not before I take a Covid test, the results of which cannot be known for a few days, but they let me into the ward anyway. Odd.

I am parked in a bed squeezed up against a window; it is the first time I have been in a hospital as a patient for many years. I suspect on the chart at the bottom of my bed they have written something like '?' to explain my reason for being there. I try to rest and sleep, urging my troubled brain and body to just relax and 'don't be so stupid,' for the umpteenth time this long afternoon and evening.

The following morning, I am woken by someone at some unearthly early hour. I need the toilet. Then I realise something very unsettling. I do not seem to be able to move my legs in any coordinated fashion that will get me off the bed. Odd.

My brain knows what to do, but there doesn't seem to be much response from my legs. Very peculiar. Much shuffling and shifting of my weight, and I am sitting on the bed and about to stand. This takes several seconds longer than it should normally. I need a mirror to check that I have not aged 40 years overnight and become a freak of nature. I work on shuffling to the toilet, which, of course, is quite some way away. The mirror confirms it. I am still 60, but clearly, something is up.

Several minutes later, I collapse onto the bed, feeling both embarrassed and confused. Breakfast (not eaten), blood pressure test and a blood test follow. My blood pressure is OK. I ask to be discharged if possible. I forget that I shall have to be seen by the doctor before that can happen. When he comes, he bears bad news. The blood test reveals I need another pint of fresh blood.

I expect him to say that I am a medical curiosity as my fuel consumption – in this case, blood usage – went through the roof in one day, and it's a miracle I am still functioning at all. He does not. The haemoglobin levels are still very low. Rats.

The cannula is inserted, and the bag drips its contents. That'll be three pints of new blood in a fortnight. Where is it all going? If I was a car, there would clearly be a fuel leak to be investigated or an inefficient engine. That's it, of course; the something up is that my engine is truly knackered. Bugger!

Halfway through the drip, I need the loo. This is going to be tricky. Not only am I going to have to concentrate inordinately on moving my legs again, but I now must simultaneously negotiate to wheel the stand containing my lifeblood in a bag. Miraculously – and despite, at one point, having to perform a ballet pirouette in slow motion in the middle of the ward to avoid strangling myself with my own new blood in a tube (no applause was forthcoming) – I make it to the toilet and back.

I call Caroline and fill her in. She offers to bring a walking stick with her when she comes to collect me. Pride will have to be swallowed as this seemingly fit and healthy 60-year-old frame accepts that it needs a stick to support it.

They let me go after more scratching of heads and confused faces. At least the shaking has stopped, but I am still finding movement inordinately complicated. I wonder if I have had a stroke, but I can talk without slurring, and I am not lopsided, just seizing up. It's all very peculiar.

Back at home, I am parked in a chair and draw the family's sympathy and wry humour when the extent of my stiff movements becomes apparent. What is also worrying is that I have lost my appetite completely and have developed an irrational need for milky tea. And I look dreadful, apparently.

That night, I made it into bed, where the sweats begin. It may be late summer but mega hot it is not, so this sudden sweating is mystifying. Maybe this is the leakage we have been waiting for and I have simply become like a saturated sponge that is releasing held moisture through every pore.

While I am not shaking, I am nonetheless exceedingly uncomfortable; I resolve to move rooms to give Caroline some respite and to avoid the flooding spreading to her side. Getting out of bed is very hard as my knees do not want to unlock. I develop a mantra that I mutter to myself: 'Step up or go home,' which my youngest son has encouraged me to repeat.

Setting off along the landing, shuffling painfully, I head for the spare room and the sofa in there to sleep on. I should be able to do this, I convince myself.

What!! Where is the sofa? Come to that, why is there no furniture in here at all?

Ah. Removal company Phase One yesterday – removing all non-essential furniture.

A sofa right now would be very essential as I am tired from the effort, and I am in pain. I need to sit down. In a moment of irrational misjudgement, I decide to lie down on the floor. To this day, I do not know why.

I try to kneel, and the slow bending of the knees, coupled with shifting my torso forwards, results in me crashing unceremoniously head-first onto the floor.

After a while, I realise this is utterly daft and I should be back in my side of the bed, which will be drying out nicely now, I guess. My brain has a clear picture of what getting up from the floor looks like and involves. I have done this millions of times.

Can I do it this night? Can I heck?

My muscles are not responding. I try to verbalise my brain's thoughts as if commanding subjects to obey. Others in the house are asleep and cannot hear the futile phrases I utter: "Come on arms, move forwards and bend. Oh, for goodness' sake, how hard can this be legs?"

Or perhaps they can and are having truly bizarre dreams

involving random sentences. It's no use. I am stuck.

I decide to call for help. My son Josh is in the room next door. I begin calling his name in a kind of muffled plea-cum-silent shout. No joy. He sleeps like a log. Brilliant.

Deciding not to summon Caroline, I settle upon the second son, who is asleep downstairs in the lounge, having come over to help with the removal process. By this time, I have twisted my body around whilst still on the floor so that I can call facing the door rather than the wall.

"Michael," I call, trying not to wake everyone but to wake Michael alone. If this works, it will be some kind of audio triumph. It does.

"What are you doing there?" he utters in disbelief when he sees me.

I can think of no rational explanation, so I confess the truth of my brain freeze and futility. Out of the kindness of his heart, he rescues me and helps me shuffle back to my now cold and damp side of the bed. Too bad. I shall endure it. Well, that was quite a night and I suspect Michael thought he was in some kind of dream himself.

When I wake on Saturday morning, I am still mystified about what is going on with my body. Moving around seems absurdly complicated and I am having to think and focus on actions that I have been doing unconsciously for well over 50 years, such as getting up from a chair and going to the toilet.

What is more, I seem to have lost flesh overnight. Yes, really. Maybe that was what was happening in bed. I was genuinely melting.

A year ago, I weighed 14 stone and 12 pounds, which was, to

be frank, too much. Over these last few months, I had noticed that I was down to around 14 stone, which was good news given that I had not really been trying to lose weight.

Today, I look at myself in the mirror and notice that my arms and legs have shrunk. What muscles I did have seem to have simply evaporated. There is sagging skin where they once were under my arms. I wonder if the lymph node biopsy sucked some of me away too with the bits they extracted. But that is unlikely, I decide. I check I am not still illuminated because of the dye and whether my pee is a lovely cerise colour, which it is not. Curious. Where does the dye go, then? Who knows?

My two sons who are present at home this weekend and have both studied sports science, seem to agree that I have simply consumed myself during the 'incident' (as I now refer to it). Weird. This is some kind of wonder of the natural world. Call Sir David Attenborough. A normal bloke consumes himself without knowing. Or perhaps it's a headline from the *Daily Star*.

Between us, we arrive at the conclusion that the connections between my brain and my muscles have been damaged by the trauma, which is why I am not responding to my thoughts.

"How come?" I ask.

"Shock," they reply.

I am going to have to teach myself how to do these simple manoeuvres again, something that I ponder upon and find utterly bizarre. This must be what happens when people have a stroke, I guess.

One thing that quickly becomes apparent is that I am going to be no use at all when it comes to packing and moving boxes ready for Phase Two of the removal men arriving on Monday. To be totally honest, I find this very hard to bear. I am someone who is always capable and on the go and while not as strong as my three sons, I can usually lift things like a box of books. Only now, I can't. I am parked in a chair like my worst nightmare image of myself in 30 years' time.

I decide not to sleep upstairs, owing to the discomfort I am still feeling in my legs and arms. Kindly, the removal people left our sofa and chairs, and I decide to settle into an armchair with an accompanying footstool for the night. Wrapped in a dressing gown and within relatively easy reach of the downstairs toilet, I try to rest.

What I had not allowed for was the sweats again, which I have since discovered are symptomatic of the illness I was later diagnosed with. Only this time, I am not lying on absorbent cotton sheets. I am lying in a leather chair. To cool down, I open the dressing gown only to find that I proceed to slide around on the chair as if someone had covered it in olive oil. This is not going to work. I resolve to dry off the moisture with the dressing gown and endure the night.

I am also confronted with another unforeseen problem – the urge to pee frequently. Now, as a man, I am aware of the issues around the prostate and have had the usual check-ups to ensure that it is not misbehaving, which have, to this point, proved clear. But I suddenly begin to have irresistible urges in the night to pee. Initially, I do the manly thing and ignore it, thinking of something else in the hope it will go away.

I learned this from numerous camping holidays when getting up in the middle of the night to go for a pee in the dark was fraught with dangers, such as guy lines, cowpats, and puddles, and therefore, was to be avoided at all costs. Only this time, it's not working. There follow numerous occasions in the night when I struggle to my feet, muttering motivational phrases to myself interspersed with swear words and shuffling to the loo for what is best described as a pathetic pee. Maybe the prostate thing has hit me. Dear God, anything else?

When sharing this dilemma with my family, we agree that something weird has gone on between my brain and my muscles and that, in not registering control over them, I have regressed to a two-year-old state when the urge to pee is instantly followed by actual pee. Only this time, I am nappy-less (thank goodness), but I have a need to move quickly (not easy as you will have gathered by now) to the toilet. This phenomenon continues for several weeks whilst my brain rediscovers its primary purpose, to govern my body and not the other way round.

That weekend, I discover that I have all but completely lost my appetite too. Can this get any more bizarre, I wonder?

Chapter 5
September 14

Today is a sad day for us as we prepare to leave our home of the last 18 years. This house has been our refuge and the only home our youngest son, Josh, has ever really known, as he was just two when we moved here. Our sons have grown up in this place, and it holds so many precious memories.

Our dog Mumford has also only known this place and the surrounding woods and walks as his territory. As a handsome and totally people-centred golden retriever, he has been one of the great characters of village life for his nine years.

Everyone knows Mumford and they address him by his name, even though we don't know their names. This morning, I am maudlin for Mumford, wondering how mean it is to take him away from everything he has ever known and to force him to start again, to make new friends and explore a new location.

I catch myself and remind myself that he is a dog and that my emotional reaction is irrational. He has been on vacation for the early days of the move and will continue to be whilst we are in limbo between homes, a period of 10 days that we had agreed to allow our buyers to move in so they could get their young son into nursery starting on the 17th, given that they were moving up from south London to our east London village.

It has been four days since the 'incident' and my mobility is still severely impacted such that I am moving slowly with the aid of a stick and not able to help with the move. I am banished to a chair in the garden, overseeing proceedings like a field general watching the battle from a remote vantage point. This makes me cross.

I am further agitated when the removal men arrive as it seems that they have come with one guy who knows what he is doing and two younger inexperienced blokes who spend much of the time making what should be simple operations seem complex and long-winded.

We must be out by lunchtime, and I am beginning to wonder if this is going to be realistic, given the pace at which they are working. My attempts to communicate urgency from the sedate position of a garden chair with a cup of coffee and a chocolate biscuit, however, do not appear to be working.

Perhaps they have seen through the cognitive dissonance or, more likely, they simply have not noticed me waving my stick or dismissed me as an old, grumpy, and slightly bonkers grandfather figure.

Miraculously – and by the skin of their teeth – they pack the huge van just in time and all that remains is for me to waddle around the house into empty rooms to say my farewell. I resolve to vacuum the lounge a bit to say that I did at least do something that day.

It is a sad day as we turn the page to a new chapter. Our belongings are being put into storage for 10 days and our numerous garden plants that are in pots are being moved to our neighbour who has agreed to look after them whilst we move into our new home.

This is very generous, as is their kind offer to lend me a walking aid contraption. This turns out to be a Zimmer frame that has wheels and a foldaway seat – presumably to park myself on when I get too tired to move further. In my darkest moment I wonder if there is some kind of portable commode that goes with it so that I can take a dump or pee in the street by lifting the foldaway seat. There isn't. Being lent this is a humiliating experience as I am not yet 90 and all my mental models associate this kind of thing with old people meandering around M&S looking for a shepherd's pie for one and some pre-grated cheese. Graciously through gritted teeth, I say how useful this will be to help me rediscover my mobility. Naturally, I hope I am never seen with it by anyone who knows me. My mother doesn't even have one and she is 87!

Just before we finally leave, I stroke the leaves of the olive tree I planted a dozen years ago as a small sapling and that has now grown into a glorious specimen some eight feet tall with fabulously iridescent pastel leaves. Last year it yielded over 200 olives. Bidding farewell to this tree and my redcurrant bush that has faithfully produced pounds and pounds of luscious redcurrants annually for over 60 years (it was a cutting that I brought from my parents' house 40 years ago and have since taken with me from home to home) is an odd way to part with a house but, at the time, feels right.

I also reflect on the profundity of me seemingly being ill and anxious just at the time when we should be optimistic about moving home. We have been trying to sell our house for almost two years and have been thwarted by a combination of inept estate agents and Brexit uncertainty. Our desire has been to move to Cambridgeshire to be near to the fledgling café art gallery business that we have been running for almost two years and, in so doing, avoid lengthy commutes up and down the M11 motorway. This moving day, therefore, should be a blend of relief and natural sadness. In many ways it is just that, whilst at the same time being a moment that feels like we have stepped off the edge of a cliff and into a void.

As I sit in the garden observing the commotion around, the dawning that something is clearly not right begins to overwhelm me. All these physical symptoms look like that they will add up to more than a mild cough or bad dose of flu. But what? And what will this mean? Am I going to pop my clogs? I feel exposed and powerless. As a Christian, I am not supposed to feel like this. I am supposed to trust in my higher being who is by my side and who looks after me. Doesn't he? Have I been abandoned?

It is at this point, honestly, that my phone rings and I see it is my dear friend Dr Nick. I had reached out to him and one or two others to tell them that I was not feeling great and was undergoing some tests. He and I go way back and have shared some wonderful experiences, lifechanging moments, and much joy. His voice is like manna to my soul just at that moment. We talk and I recount some of the nonsense that has been happening to me in the hospital, laughing a lot as we do so often when we meet.

Just then, he proceeds to read out to me one of my own poems that he has read in my recently published book of poems. This short piece is entitled 'Brokenness' and is a reflection on the astounding work done by the NHS. Quite whether he had planned to read it to me before he called, I do not know. What I do know is that I fall apart there and then. When my wife and son come to find out what is going on, I dissolve into a deep sobbing that I have not known for many years. Just as my body had gone into an all-consuming shock reaction a few days earlier, I am now consumed by this emotional tidal wave. A wave not of panic or fear but a wave of pure peace and assurance that is so far beyond my human understanding or sense-making. I am convinced it is of God. I have not and will not be abandoned, it seems. Mind you, I am still moving with the speed of a three-toed sloth.

After much deliberation and, mindful of having to attend some tests in Harlow most likely, we have booked into a hotel just outside Cambridge for a few nights as a treat. It has a spa. The three of us; Josh, having decided that a free stay in a posh hotel is better than student digs, heads there that afternoon. Mercifully, we have been able to book rooms that are on the ground floor, so I do not have to negotiate lots of stairs with the smoothness of a bookcase making its own way up the steps. How much embarrassment can a man take, after all?

The venue does not disappoint, and the weather is hot and sunny, which lifts our spirits. It also has a good selection of comfy chairs. I have discovered the almost Monty Pythonesque need to utter the phrase 'fetch the comfy chair' (reference a sketch about the Spanish Inquisition if you are confused).

Never have I been so fixated on the plumpness of cushions. This is because my melting process seems to have focused on my buttocks such that they have literally vanished. I cannot actually see them of course (it's hard to see your own buttocks), but I sure can tell that they are not as fleshy as they were a couple of weeks ago. I am left with some sinews clinging on to the bones in my bum and the most peculiar of sensations when I sit in a chair.

I can best describe the profound discomfort of sitting on a hard surface as like the spine-chilling sense one gets when someone grates a knife blade across a metal tray, or when you are invited to sit on a stone wall that has recently frozen to minus 10 degrees. It's not nice. I find I must move my bottom gingerly from side to side.

September has coincided with many restrictions on movement and coming together having been relaxed by the UK government in a bid to kick-start the economy following the devastation wrought by the initial lockdowns to limit the spread of Covid-19. This means that there are a few people about although not many guests in the hotel. I am relieved by this as my embarrassment when walking around will not be seen by so many people.

Now, quite why I should be concerned by this is, of course, ridiculous, as none of the people in this hotel know me from Adam. Nonetheless, I am bothered as my human frailty is dawning on me.

The spa was a factor in booking this hotel for our three-night stay, so we decide to go and use the pool. Due to Covid, we must book a time slot when we can pretty much have it to ourselves and, armed with swimming costumes and flip-flops, we make our way there, stick in hand in my case.

In normal circumstances, people change quickly and move smoothly from the changing rooms through to the pool. I, however, am concerned I will slip over, given my stiffness of movement, so I waddle gingerly into the pool room, which is very hot. I had wondered if I would be allowed to take a walking stick in with me and I decide to do so. I walk nonchalantly past reception to try not to draw attention to myself. I get away with it. Phew!

Gradually, it dawns on me that I need to negotiate the steps down into the pool and, given how I have been with stairs and steps of late, this appears daunting. I wish at this point for a flume or slide that I could simply flop onto and glide gracefully down into the water. No such luck. This is a posh spa, for goodness' sake, not Butlins. Undeterred, I glide effortlessly down the shiny and slippery steps.

I wish.

Accompanied by much groaning and phrases like 'oh my goodness' and 'oh dear,' gripping onto the metal handrail and fortunately observed by nobody other than Caroline and Josh, I make it into the wonderful world of weightlessness. It's mercifully warm.

As fortune would have it, my youngest son Josh is studying sports therapy at university and is in his third year, which should have been a placement with a rugby club in Melbourne, Australia. Thwarted by the global pandemic and barred from travelling to magical Oz, he has nonetheless found a worthy substitute placement project in the form of his suddenly decrepit father. A sad disappointment, to be honest, not unlike the Wizard of Oz himself. Hurrah!

He tackles my time in the pool as if I was an elite performance athlete desperate to get back on the pitch.

"Just start walking," he entreats me.

Like an injured dressage horse recovering from a steeplechase, I set off in a kind of comical prancing movement, lifting my legs and bending my knees to try and get them moving properly. I feel like some idiot guy practicing a pseudo-walking on the moon routine as I make my way towards the other end. But it does help. I can move my legs and arms more easily whilst my son, clearly relishing the opportunity to try out hydrotherapy on someone real, tells me that my brain will start to build some muscle memory. I rest at the end and move my legs whilst supporting myself on the side of the pool. Then, horror of horrors, another person enters the pool. She is a lady of advancing years who proceeds to swim up and down whilst glancing over at us and smiling a warm and caring smile.

Later, Josh tells me that when he left the pool and encountered the lady, she asked him if he was my carer! For goodness' sake, I must clearly have aged overnight still further, and my mobility challenges are presenting a scene of utter helplessness. Sadly, this is not far from the truth. He laughs and tells her that he is my son and that I am much younger than I clearly look or behave just now.

Whilst we try and relax to enjoy our stay in the hotel, we have another appointment to fulfil. This has been arranged by the hospital in Harlow, which is now 50 miles away, and is the latest diagnostic test I must undergo.

A bone marrow biopsy. What fun. I am imagining what this could possibly involve and what the unforeseen consequences of this might be. I put it to the back of my mind, choosing instead to focus on pool gymnastics – walking and swimming gently. But there is no getting away from the fact that we must set off for yet more new adventures.

As with all modern hospitals, the Princess Alexandra Hospital in Harlow is like a large village at the centre of which is one huge ugly building, presumably built in the 1960s or 1970s and enlarged through a series of bolted-on extensions that bear no resemblance to the original building. It's a bit like when, as a child, we would build Lego buildings and then add round bits or triangular bits to them, or a blue brick tower next to a yellow one. Maybe that is what goes on with contemporary hospital design – it's merely an extension of childhood games with Lego.

Around this central Soviet-style faceless block are myriads of smaller buildings that presumably were once cottages or sheds and have now been turned into pathology labs or foot clinics. I am relieved that the nuclear unit is housed inside the main 'reactor building' and not a converted 10 x 8 shed. Anyway, we have been asked to report to the Cancer Unit that is housed in one such outbuilding. An auspicious name for a unit and one that bothers me, understandably.

Naturally, this takes us a while to find and once I am dropped off, Caroline then must find a parking space, which, as we all know, in a hospital is like searching for the Ark of the Covenant itself. Who knows where it is?

Inside the Cancer Unit, I approach the window to announce my arrival. But there is nobody there.

A few chairs are positioned around the place in a seemingly totally random pattern to accommodate social distancing. I stand at the glass partition not sure whether I should go for a wander or wait. I look for a handy counterbell – you know, like the ones that shops and reception desks used to have – only to realise, of course, that such a thing would be a death trap surface for the virus. I shuffle into the toilet instead to kill some time. When I emerge, a person has appeared behind the window, and I go to her to state my business.

I am clearly mumbling through my mask and given that there is an inch-thick screen between us and about three feet of space, I get no acknowledgment of my name. Mind you, when she speaks to me, I cannot easily decipher what she is saying either. One thing that this pandemic is clearly going to do is to make the whole planet increase the normal human voice volume by several decibels as we have learned to shout through our masks and these screens. I dutifully raise my voice to a mild shout, leaving scope for a total holler should it be required.

"I'm here for a bone marrow biopsy!"

Whether she can hear the sheer terror in my voice, I am not sure, but I think I have concealed it well enough as she does not offer me any kind of sympathy whatsoever.

I was expecting, "Oh, you poor thing," or "Don't worry, it's a walk in the park."

Instead, it's simple, "Take a seat around the corner and someone will come for you."

When I am invited into a small room by a kindly nurse, I am introduced to a doctor who greets me with such disarmingly gentle tones that I immediately see through his ploy. This is to just relax me ahead of the nightmare that awaits. Surprisingly, Caroline is allowed in with me. Ha, my air of utterly pathetic fear has paid off, a bit like when we used to have to sit alongside our boys for their first-ever haircut at the barbers or trip to the dentist.

The doctor, who has an Arabic name and a warm smile, sits me down and talks me through what he is going to do.

We are going to take a sample of your spinal fluid and remove a tiny piece of bone so that they can be analysed for any signs of disease, he explains. We will numb the area first so you won't feel any pain as I make a small incision and go in with a shovel to dig around for the bone.

He might as well have said shovel to be frank as I have already worked out that spinal fluid is likely to be located around my spine and that bones are, like my spine, not on the surface.

It might feel a bit strange, he adds, as he will have to exert some pressure to get through the outer layers to my hip bone.

Rats!

I had hoped it could have been done with, shall we say, one of my fingers, as that's bone too, isn't it?

I enquire timidly if I might have some knock-out drops, too, as the previous and only digging biopsy of part of me resulted in a total meltdown of my mind, body and spirit, which I would very much like to avoid this time.

He says he could but would prefer not to as that would require me to stay in the hospital for quite a while to ensure I have recovered properly and, because it is already 4 pm, I would have to be transferred to another part of the hospital as this unit shuts at around 5 pm.

You don't say! The deja vue is so heavily laden with irony that I stare in disbelief at Caroline. Note to self – book hospital appointments in the mornings from now on.

He reckons I will be fine with the local anaesthetic. Despite it being really hot in here, I resolve to show up or go home!

Once again, I must lie on my side, this time presenting my buttocks rather than my armpits. Perhaps he will comment with derision at the now shrunken bum that I offer up, but he doesn't. Caroline holds my hand to reassure me. How tables turn, as these last couple of weeks have seen her do this quite a bit. I have rarely been in hospital on account of myself, but have held her hand in reassurance, I hope, during the four instances of childbirth she has endured.

To quote Pink Floyd, my hips and bum are now 'comfortably numb.' I cannot see what he is doing thankfully, but I can certainly feel it. He was right when he said he would have to use some pressure

41

to reach the bone and then even more to remove a tiny piece of it. Unnervingly though, it is only pressure and not pain that I sense.

Once it is all over and he has drained some surprisingly vivid pink fluid from my spine area (I knew it, the dye is still in me and was cerise all along!) and a couple of pieces of my hip bone, I thank him sincerely for his skill and warmheartedness. His spirit is a gentle and kind one which is exactly what I needed to allay my fears. God has been with me. Now we must wait for the diagnosis that will come in just a few days. Oh my.

September is warm and sunny, as it so often is, and they are playing cricket later in the year than ever to catch up on a fragmented season. Up until a year or so ago, I played for my local village side in Havering. Our ground is truly unique, perched atop a hill on the edge of London that overlooks a huge swathe of the south-east.

The postage stamp-sized ground is bounded on one side by a road and the other three sides by fields that fall away sharply. This geography means that we need a sight screen on the boundary near the road to allow us to see the red ball emerging from the giant wall of dark green trees and hedges on the other side of the road, but no such screen at the other end of the ground as the sky itself provides the backdrop above a truly spectacular panorama of Essex, Kent, and East London.

We do, of course, hit the occasional passing vehicle a glancing blow with a ball that has been hit well and clears the boundary. Mostly, there is no significant damage, although I do recall one chap parked up in the layby on the other side of the road to watch the game with his window open, and having to mention to him that if he spent the whole afternoon there directly behind the play, there was a reasonable chance that he might get a ball smack on the chops. He moved and just a few minutes later, a ball did zing its way over, bouncing just where his car had been.

We also lose a lot of balls in the surrounding vegetation, an occupational hazard of village cricket. The most we lost in one game was nine balls, and, as captain at the time, it was my job to have a kit bag full of replacement balls. That day, a rather unsophisticated batsman from Hullbridge simply clubbed his way to a large score by smiting the ball in a baseball fashion over the boundary. We would have needed a ground a full 30 yards bigger in diameter to curtail him and his rather keen eye for a slog. Ah, village cricket is not for the purists amongst us. My ball bag was exhausted by the end of his innings, and I recall that we played our innings using a rather ragged ball; that was all I had left. We lost.

I have missed cricket this year and I am contemplating whether I will ever be able to turn out again as my 60s advance. I do hope so, but my body may have other ideas. Right now, my muscles have lost all sense of their purpose and I doubt I could pick up a cricket bat and play a shot. This depresses me.

When you have been naturally fit all your life, able to play football with the kids and able to play a full game of cricket and spend 40 overs behind the stumps as a wicketkeeper, which was where I found myself often, to be stopped in your tracks seems so alien and debilitating. I am frustrated by this sudden demise in my physical condition.

My mind dwells on the awful events a couple of years back when one of our cricket club's brightest and cheeriest members, Dave Roe, was struck down by liver cancer. He was in his mid-40s. He was gone in just three weeks! He was told the cancer had developed so far and fast that he should be taken to a hospice immediately as there was nothing that could be done. He chose to go home and spend his final moments with his family.

I reflect on these matters over this week as I try to make sense of what might be the reason for my malaise. There are moments when I catastrophise and begin to ponder the worst scenarios. Maybe I am like Dave Roe and will have only a few more weeks to live. It doesn't feel like that, but then I was completely unaware that something was afoot. Yet I also have moments of unreal peace as I remind myself that I am blessed. I am alive and kicking, and I am surrounded and supported by people who love me genuinely and generously.

Chapter 6
September 18

We're checking out to stay at an Airbnb. We have been at the hotel for four nights and have rented the Airbnb for a week. It's quite close to the middle of Cambridge. This will allow us to be on hand should I need to visit the hospital. It is, however, on the first floor we discover, so I am going to have to find a way of going up and down stairs more fluently.

Time to break out the old person's mobility thingy that I have been lent as I make my way into the building. I soon realise that trying to use a device that has wheels on two of its feet whilst going up stairs is likely to end in complete disaster, so we ditch that idea in favour of the stick that Caroline so kindly bought me to remind me how rapidly I have presumably aged.

Having lugged everything upstairs and left quite an assortment of our belongings in the car, we explore the flat. It's very new. The building isn't, but the flat has been recently refurbished, which means that it is pretty much white everywhere. There's a nice lounge area with a dining table and chairs in the corner, a small but tidy kitchen and two bedrooms with the now customary hanging rails from Ikea. This will be OK.

My appetite has still vanished which means that, for Caroline, planning meals for us is impossible. One minute, I can relish the prospect of fish and chips and then, when presented with them on the plate, my mind goes blank and decides that I do not need the food nor like it. Breakfast cereal, though, is strangely acceptable to my brain and pallet, as is yoghurt, soft fruit, fruit juice and warm milky tea. Oh well.

My son recommends something to give me energy.

"Excellent," I say. "What are we talking about?"

Apparently, it is possible to buy something that is akin to an energy drink but is actually an energy gel that famous sports people consume in vast amounts during matches and training. Packaged in a pouch, once I acquire four of these things, it seems that one simply has to squeeze it and suck. I decide to mix my flavours and have gone for two orange ones and two minty ones. Eagerly, I go in on the first orange one.

Occasionally, in life, one is presented with new sensations that nothing that has gone before has prepared you for, like the first time you ride a death-defying roller coaster or fly long-haul in First Class. Exhilarating perhaps. Inconceivably different from the normal run-of-the-mill experience. Well, this is one such moment.

Not only is the substance (I cannot think of any other appropriate noun) the colour of nuclear-eradiated Irn Bru, but its taste resembles what I imagine an environmentally-friendly floor cleaner to taste like – pretending to be nice, but you know it really contains unimaginable chemical concoctions. Worse, though, is the texture. I can best describe it as like a three-day-old wallpaper paste – not quite fully set but not runny enough to use.

On the first mouthful, my face is a picture of utter disbelief. I gag. Surely there has been some mistake. Perhaps we are supposed to have heated it first, frozen it, or fried it. Goodness only knows. What I do know is that I have never had anything in my mouth quite so unexpectedly vile. Caroline laughs. I decide to challenge my narrow assumptions of life and go for another portion.

Nope, clearly, I have been given a pouch of Uncle Ben's curried rice from the Chernobyl Nuclear Power Plant staff canteen. It has gone off in a truly dramatic fashion. Energy gel, it must surely be. Potable, edible, palatable, it is not. I rush to get water to dilute the poison. Rush, you understand, in the loosest of ways, as I cannot get up quickly enough myself before I pass out from the shock, so I simply holler: "Water! I need water!"

We decide to pass on this for a day and try again tomorrow in the hope that my body can embrace the modern world. Sadly, the minty version is just as indescribable. This is genuinely reconstituted Flash or battery acid. More gagging and statements of incredulity lead to complete surrender. I may need some clever ways of consuming energy, but I think I will revert to a Mars Bar and leave this stuff to Mo Farah and Andy Murray.

We venture out for some takeaways and arrange to meet our son Nick and his dog for a meal in a pub garden on the banks of the River Cam, famous for giving great views of the Cambridge Bumps rowing festival that we have attended and in which Nick and his wife Susie have participated. I'm getting used to the walking wheely thing and I don't feel quite so ridiculous with it.

A gentle walk across a bridge over the River Cam takes us to some meadows popular with walkers, runners, cyclists and cows.

Yes, cows.

This is common land and cows are allowed to roam freely, to lounge around under trees and to leave their pats everywhere. The path alongside the river is just wide enough for cyclists and pedestrians, although I am discovering that cyclists in Cambridge are of the supremely confident genre, verging on over-confident. But then the city does encourage cycling as if we were in Holland itself. Here I am, moving gracefully and ever so slowly on my frame, when I am presented with what seems to be a conflagration ahead of me.

A couple of young mothers with buggies and some children in tow are approached by a herd of cattle, granted, slow-moving too. The herd has decided to up sticks and find some shade. The mothers are wary of the cattle, so they try to adjust their trajectory but cannot because doing so would mean moving into the lane for cyclists, who might simply mow them down. The other route is fraught with cowpat danger. If you have ever had really small children, you will be thinking exactly what I am right now.

Into this melange wanders some old chap with a stroller and his wife, who is carrying a shopping bag and a camping chair. It is like a scene from a movie played out in slow motion, as nobody seems to be unduly phased.

I decide the best option is to pause and sit. The stroller thing (there is clearly an actual noun for this, but it is unknown to me) has an inbuilt seat, which is a tad firm and, for all I know, hides a self-inflating commode when it is raised. Caroline graciously offers to perch on the thing and allow me the relative comfort of the camping chair. We make camp under a tree and watch the scene that could only really happen in England unfold.

Unwritten rules and some genetic programming for cows lead to a gloriously seamless series of manoeuvres that allow the cows to move effortlessly through the now-gathered crowd of people whilst the occasional cyclist weaves his way like a threaded needle in a piece of needlework. I muse on how the famous Cambridge poets of yore would have described this quintessentially English summer scene.

We make it as far as a pub and I need refreshment. It is closed for a private function and the wonderful terrace of seats overlooking the river is sadly out of bounds. The late summer heat has parched me, so I try to play the poor old man walking with the aid of a strange, marooncoloured frame thingy card. No joy, but there is a small independent pop-up coffee retailer nearby, presumably for the occasion of the pub being closed. Furnished with lemonade and seated watching rowers in boats, cyclists, roller skaters, mums with kids on bikes and dog walkers aplenty, I find my spirits lifted and I am almost joyful.

The flat we have rented comes with wi-fi that allows me to hold some calls with work colleagues. When I explain what has been going on, albeit as briefly as I can, their incredulity is palpable.

"How can someone lose so much body weight overnight?"

"What do you mean you can't walk properly?"

I resist telling them about my nightly escapades.

My body is clearly in a state of complete disturbance on so many fronts, not least of which is a complete inability to sleep at the proper time and in the proper place. Each night, I get into bed, but I am increasingly doubtful that I will be able to sleep. My bones ache and my legs are pulsing as if an electric current has been passed through them. I fidget incessantly. We try more pillows behind me to make me comfortable and some under my legs too. I feel like the Princess and the Pea (if you remember that fairy tale, great; if not, I am sorry, as the analogy will mean nothing).

49

We try music and sounds. I fire up Spotify and link it to my Bluetooth speaker to play some worship songs that are OK for a while but soon lose their potency. I try soothing sounds, including waves. Apparently, the sound of the sea is supposed to induce rest and help sleep. Maybe if it is accompanied by a gently rolling boat, that may be true. In my case, it merely induces the need for the loo again and again.

Turning to the loo, or should I say bathroom, it is a large, recently refurbished room at the end of the corridor. But here's the thing: it was either done by some very small people or by someone who carried the whole nautical theme a bit too far. It has shells and boaty things all around.

The sink is miniature and narrow, and the wrong size for the water pressure and taps, meaning that when the tap is lifted, it leads to an eruption of water into the sink that cannot contain it and the water simply splashes everywhere. It takes me several days of splashed trousers and damp legs before I master it.

Then there is the toilet. I have never thought about it before, but there is an optimum size for a toilet, one that allows the average bum to rest comfortably. This one is not optimum. It is narrow, more of a squished oval shape. I find it awkward, and, given my recently reduced bum padding, it is an uncomfortable experience, akin to taking up position on what amounts to something only slightly larger than a sardine tin.

As previously mentioned, my brain-to-bladder and bowel communication is, at best, patchy, which, in simple terms, means I am visiting this overly large bathroom with tiny fittings scattered around the edges more often than I would like.

The shower works in the opposite manner to the sink in that it produces a very narrow needle-like jet of hot water that I must be careful not to get onto my lower back where I have the wound from the bone marrow biopsy. I would rather avoid doing the whole procedure again using a high-pressure shower jet.

I suspect that the bathroom was originally designed to be fitted in a hobbit house or narrow boat and someone thought, 'That'll do.' I resolve to make them 'do' for the week or so.

When it comes to moving into our new house, the anticipation grips us as the week progresses. September 25 finally arrives and so do the removal men for the first unloading. It is fair to say that unloading a removal vehicle is a whole lot quicker than loading it.

As with the emptying of our former house, I am resigned to being utterly useless in the re-filling process. Instead of the garden, I take up a seat in the small study to give out instructions as to where pieces of furniture and boxes are to be taken. My sense of fraudulent authority is not lost on me. The whole process goes very smoothly, and we await the second lorry coming on the following Monday for the next batch. I though, will not be there for that as I am due to attend the Princess Alexandra Hospital in Harlow to see the consultant, presumably for the results of my tests.

Chapter 7
September 28

My youngest son Josh chauffeurs me the 50 miles to Harlow or, to be precise, the outbuildings that form the cancer unit, whilst Caroline marshals the removals. The two of us are taken into a small room where we are greeted by another new face, Doctor Al, and a nurse, both of whom have warm smiles and gentle manners. Doctor Al is to become a regular feature in my life, and I have not shared his full name out of courtesy.

I am asked how I am.

"Okay," I say, although clearly, that is a lie, given that I shuffled in with the aid of a walking stick.

"Why are you using the stick?" Dr Al asks.

"It's a long story," I say. "Involving an extreme panic attack during the lymph node biopsy."

"That's unusual."

"Maybe," I reply.

He has papers in front of him and, without beating around any bush, he comes straight out with it.

"We have discussed your case in the haematology unit and the results of the lymph node biopsy and the bone marrow biopsy seem to indicate that you have a lymphoplasmacytic lymphoma. Probably Waldenström macroglobulinemia."

I am stunned, not least because anyone who can actually say these words is clearly a genius, but more so because I have no idea what I have just heard other than it doesn't sound like joyous news.

I was expecting something like this, given that the discussions during the tests were heading this way and that I was being invited to see him in the Cancer Unit. Nonetheless, I am dazed.

Living in the UK in the 21st century, I am acutely aware of how common cancer is in our population. My brother developed a brain tumour when he was just 43 of such a veracious type that he was given just a few months to live. Regular radiotherapy sessions followed, and he was forced to leave his job as a postman that he had held for 25 years.

As a family, we watched him discover new hobbies and find a new circle of friends who were fellow sufferers and carers in the daycare centre he attended. But his balance began to deteriorate dramatically along with his eyesight in his left eye. It was his vision that was one of the first signs something was wrong. He had walked into things on his left-hand side and, when he drove his Post Office van gently into something he had not seen, it became clear he needed to be investigated. The Glioblastoma Multiform had grown around his optic nerve and required a major brain operation.

Twenty years ago, I had been busy both with my work and living in London with my family. My parents were tormented as their eldest son fell apart before them. He lived at home as he had never had the confidence to move out, and his life from the day he was born had been tough as he was born with a major intestinal condition that required surgery throughout his early years. For me, I experienced it at something of a distance until the last few weeks of his life when I was needed to support my folks. His consultant, a lovely Christian physician, told me that the tumour was almost impossible to eradicate from his brain, rather like dropping a few spots of red paint into a tin of white paint. It grew back and basically messed with his brain big time. He became confused, lost his balance, and other parts of his brain shut down. He died at the age of 48 in 2004.

So, I had been touched by the 'Big C.'

Furthermore, I had completed a consulting assignment with Cancer Research UK, developing their leadership population between 2013 and 2016, which brought me face-to-face with the extraordinary people working to develop cures for cancer and those raising millions of pounds to fund the research. I knew then about some of the radical new ways of treating cancer being discovered but, of course, never once did I think that this would touch me so very closely.

For what seems like ages, I don't say anything.

It was probably only a few seconds.

I realise that my youngest son is with me in the room and must be phased by this too. Strangely, I don't feel any sense of doom or panic. I suspect this is because I had been mulling over what the possible diagnosis could be for several weeks and now, to have it confirmed and given a name – unpronounceable and instantly forgettable as it is – is kind of proper. Maybe it's what happens when in shock, a sort of surreal state of suspended reality. I ask him to elaborate on the disease a bit more, basically, explain what it is that he has just said.

"It's a blood cancer," he says.

Ah.

Again, for what feels like a slow-motion moment in a film, I am wondering if this means I shall be departing this world quite soon.

Anyone who says that they don't think like this when they get this kind of diagnosis is lying through their teeth. Of course you do. Unless you are a dolphin, we have all heard of cancer and we know what it means. Dolphins, by the way, don't suffer from cancer at all, I think, or at least it has never been found in them. So, they are either brilliant at hiding it and parking all the sick dolphins in some acute dolphin hospital somewhere, or it is true.

Naturally, I broach the obvious subject of treatment and what this all means for me.

The good news, he says, is that it is treatable with chemotherapy, and he proceeds to tell me that he has talked about this with his colleagues, and they have agreed on a course of action, presumably some kind of witches' brew, and I am not thrilled by this prospect one bit.

I watched my brother treated with drugs and radiotherapy and it was not an uplifting picture. It would mean me coming into the hospital in Harlow every fortnight or month for prolonged sessions of intravenous poison that is essentially going to spray machine gun fire and kill everything inside me, good or bad, and, in so doing, there is a good chance that the nasty deformed blood cells will get caught in the crossfire.

I mention that I now live in Huntingdon.

Ah.

At this point, I find some courage amidst the numbness and ask if I can go private as I have been paying for private medical insurance for years without ever using it. My boys have used it for various knee surgeries or eye operations, so I figure it's pay-up time, perhaps.

"Oh, that's good," he says.

It will mean I can be treated with a whizzy new drug therapy that targets only the offending blood cells and zaps them to death. The sniper option.

Apparently, the NHS won't fund this anyway.

Oh, I muse. This sounds like it's expensive – the Harrods option – while the witches' brew chemo is presumably the Tesco solution. The Poundstretcher treatment is probably to drink neat vodka or poitin (pronounced 'potcheen'; a lethal Irish spirit made from potatoes) and hope to dilute the blood. Or, as Donald Trump once advocated, drink bleach.

The doctor decides to make a call to his friendly dealer, I mean pharmacist, at the private hospital to enquire if I can get this treatment paid for by my health insurer. They agree it sounds like I should be able to, although I will need to sort that out with them. Ibrutinib is the name of the drug. Sounds a bit too close to Irn Bru for my liking – maybe it's orange and made of girders.

To cover all the bases, the delightfully warm and friendly nurse gives me her card and says I can call her at any time, just in case I end up going with the Tesco option. I hope to God I don't. Dr Al says that the drug treatment means that I can get the disease to a managed level – remission – and that I can live normally with it for years.

I wonder.

Would that be like living with a wasps' nest in the corner of your living room, perhaps? They won't hurt you if you don't bother them, but how do you carry on life and ignore the buzzing? I am, though, heartened that it seems I won't need to get my affairs in order just yet. I need to arrange to see him at the private hospital on Friday when he is based there, and we can arrange the exchange of drugs for money.

"OK," I say. "I will be there."

Throughout all of this, Josh has been remarkably calm. I sense, though, that he is profoundly shocked behind his calm exterior, but I am awestruck by his maturity for a 21-year-old who has just witnessed his father being told he is very ill. I thank God for this. He goes to collect the car and we head back to the new house to consider what has just happened and talk it through with Caroline.

I am not sure whether it would be easier to confess to being a spy for the Russians than to have to call people and tell them that I have a terrible disease. The result is the same – momentary stunned silence. I might try this one day when I am asked what I do for a living just to see the effect.

Back at the new house, we arrange a family WhatsApp that evening and I tell all the boys what has been discovered in me with the same matter-of-factness as if I was informing them that I have an advanced case of deathwatch beetle. None of us has much idea of what it all means or could mean. I imagine that they are upset and anxious. We pray together as a family and joke about the perfect timing of all this during a house move and a pandemic, although we are, thankfully, in a period of relative freedom of movement.

Caroline is, as always, unflustered.

She doesn't flap about anything although she would have to

be utterly inhumane not to be feeling unsettled and anxious. We've both just turned 61 and have been through our fair share of tough moments. In our early years of marriage, we knew times of plenty and times of famine. We knew joy and sadness.

The joy of having our first-born child, Nicholas, in 1985, and then the desolation of losing our second-born child, Christopher, in 1988. His life of just 11 weeks was normal in every way until the day he died, unexplained other than the official terminology – sudden infant death syndrome (SIDS), more commonly known as cot death.

Then, there was the joy of welcoming our third son, Michael, over Christmas in 1988, followed by the constant anxiety of his early months checking to see if he was breathing every night when he went to sleep. The surprise of our fourth son Joshua's arrival followed in December 1999.

Over the years, our Christian faith has kept us balanced and helped us make a degree of sense of our circumstances. And yet, this is another matter, perhaps. Growing up as a young believer, I was once told that if God wants to get our attention, he must only do one of three things – target our finances, our children, or our health.

Bingo! That was a full house for me then.

Clearly, I am hard of hearing when it comes to God. Or maybe God has it in for me. Who knows? But the days following the confirmed diagnosis are strange, to say the least. I am wrestling with the still clumsy immobility in my muscles whilst now finding a way to come to terms with a disease that has come from nowhere to invade me.

One morning, as the sun floods our lounge with warmth, I am

listening to some of my favourite music, and I turn to 'Intermezzo' by Pietro Mascagni, a popular, profoundly simple and yet glorious melody that I love.

Without warning, I become overwhelmed with a feeling of deep ease and love such as I have rarely known. My whole being sobs uncontrollably. Not a welling up of sadness or feeling of pain but one of being held. Loved. I am aware that I do not have any sense of fear. Surely, I should have, given what we know and assume about cancer. But I don't. Is this of God, this peace that makes no rational sense?

Later that week, I got a call from a friend who is a doctor and whose daughter is one of my son's best friends and whom we have watched grow into a wonderful young woman now married to my son's best friend. Apparently, he is driving around the north coast of Scotland on holiday in his camper van with his wife, and Annette has told him about me. I tell him the bizarre details of the story.

Although a general practitioner rather than a haematology expert, he knows his stuff and is aware of the things that I have. He reassures me that the new type of drug that I am likely to be given is one of a family of targeted treatments that are proving effective. But most importantly, he affirms my stance that 'as I did not invite this disease into me, I am serving it notice and want it gone completely.' In his experience, my friend says that maintaining a positive attitude, combined with advances in science and the healing power of the Christian faith (which he shares with me), can make the difference between succumbing and surviving. He prays with me.

I share his view that healing comes in many ways. Rarely do we see the supernatural, although it does occur – there are examples from all around the world – and perhaps we should be more expectant

59

of this. Who knows? However, my personal faith embraces that my God brings about the healing of the body, mind and soul through the skills of people who have trained as doctors, health professionals, mental nurses, counsellors and coaches. And friends. The warmth of the love of friends and family carries real power. Knowing we are held in care and concern edifies our well-being, a key component of physical and mental health.

For me, I am amazed by how many people are with me on this journey through their love and support. I decide to post on Facebook that I am not well and that it has stunned me. Moreover, I write that I am determined to kick this disease out of my body with God's help. Whether this confidence is a kind of denial of reality, I am unsure. Psychologists might suggest this is the case, and I feel self-aware enough to agree that it could be, but that I am also looking to be as positive as I can be when faced with an unpronounceable potential death sentence. I do, however, have some important questions to raise with Dr Al.

Chapter 8
October 2

Near Bishop's Stortford, Dr. Al has requested I visit him at a different hospital as a private patient. I will need to visit him there and undergo another blood test, as well as receive some plasma. I'm not entirely sure why, but it seems I'm running low on plasma as well.

Caroline drives me as I am still not able to trust my muscles that are having to relearn and reconnect with my brain. It would be a tricky conversation to be having with a traffic officer who pulls me over for speeding when my defence was simply that the communication between my eyes, brain and feet seems to have been medically interrupted temporarily. Plausible? Maybe not. I might try it one day.

The hospital has a dedicated oncology unit, which can be approached via a secret path around the back of the hospital and through a door in the French windows. In addition, and this is extremely helpful, there are dedicated parking spaces for people attending the cancer unit and these are conveniently located next to the secret path.

It still takes us a while to find this at the rear of an overflow car park and next to what seems to be a fixed camper van parked up on a grassy area. I say fixed because a tell-tale blue power cable is running from said mobile home to a window in the side of the hospital. I am curious as to why this is. Maybe the camper van is powering the hospital, or some shrewd consultant has set up his own cheaper version of a clinic. I shall never know although, on one visit, I did encounter a lady who was spectacularly lost and was trying to get into the camper van thinking it was the Covid-19 test centre. Granted, the signs in the car park are a tad vague, but it would be a stretch to see an army of testers in their PPE squashed into a two-berth mobile home.

We ring the bell on the back door and are greeted warmly, invited in, and enter a strangely calm and remarkably empty ward. I have, of course, been used to being seen in a classically old NHS hospital that has grown by bolting on assorted blocks, sheds, and lean-tos. This place is amazing. Bright and spacious. I am expected and shown an exceptionally comfortable chair in my own booth. There are three other chairs here too, a TV monitor and various items of hospital paraphernalia. Caroline is allowed to sit in a slightly less comfortable chair in the corner.

To take some blood from me, the nurse tries in vain to coax some out of my left arm and a vein that she thinks will yield. It does not. I tell her that I am officially a slow bleeder and that, given I have been told I have some unpronounceable blood disorder, I kind of think I need to hold on to as much as I have in the hope that some of it might work properly. After all, she could be taking the only good stuff I have, as I cannot intentionally give her access to the bad stuff alone. She decides I need to warm up.

Odd, I think, as she produces a tiny electric blanket that she wraps around my arm. What a great thing!

After 10 minutes of this, I feel my left arm slowly warming, and she comes to check if I am done, cooked all the way through, I guess. And the only way to check that is, of course, to stick a needle in me again and see if there will be blood. This time, there is.

Over the years of having blood tests or needles stuck into me,

I have learned to look the other way just in case I pass out again. I have no idea how much she extracts or what colour it is; perhaps a tad watery, I suspect. Once this is over, she then tells me she is going to put a cannula into my now suitably toasted hand for the plasma. The slow dripping lasts for the best part of three hours during which time I have appreciated the recliner chair greatly. Caroline has not appreciated the more utilitarian corner seat.

I remind her that during childbirth – we've been through this four times – she got to lie down while I sat in uncomfortable chairs for hours on end. This does not land well. I guess the pain of childbirth is pretty extreme, even compared to the unpronounceable blood thing that has left me 'just a little out of breath.'

We are offered tea, biscuits and a choice of ham sandwiches or a hot option for lunch. We go safe and tuck into some very acceptable ham sandwiches. Whilst there, other cancer sufferers enter through the back door and take up a booth rather like they would their favourite table in a restaurant. These folk are regulars. Some do not look well.

They are greeted affectionately by the staff and, as they too are wired up to drips, presumably of the chemotherapy kind, the conversations range from the normal everyday stuff through to explicit details of weight, bowel movements, nausea and all the unpleasant aspects of being a human being who is suffering. I realise that I do not know quite how to feel about this moment. It would appear I am equally unwell, but to be honest, I don't feel as bad as clearly some do. Should I? Perhaps I will when it all catches up on me. What are my chances of beating this thing, by the way?

A short while later I can put these questions directly to Dr Al.

In the main part of the hospital, I pass security scrutiny – it is a Covid world, and hospitals are prime locations for spreading the virus – but Caroline is forced to sit in the car. Only patients are allowed inside, apparently, although when I do get into Dr Al's consulting room, he simply runs roughshod over the rules and tells them to let her in, too. I am very glad of this. Being physically fragile, I am also noticing a lurking mental anxiety.

Amid the global Covid pandemic, hundreds of people are being challenged to the core of their humanity in scenarios far worse than mine. Unable to be close to loved ones who are struggling desperately for life's breath and unable to explain why this thing has befallen them or their loved ones. Lonely and frightened. It is the curse of 2020.

Dr Al shares with me that my blood test reveals a still meagre haemoglobin level of 78, and more worryingly, he now has the actual bone marrow biopsy results that reveal that my personal stock of bone marrow is 90% infected with this disease.

Blimey.

Struggling for something to say in response, I can only muster: "That doesn't sound good."

"No, it isn't," he confirms. "But we have now caught it."

"Are we late with this?" I ask.

"Well, it is a very slow-developing disease, so it's been happening over quite some time."

Without actually saying it, he kind of infers that I have done well to not be dead yet. Good news, though, the drug treatment is highly effective, and he sees no reason why it cannot be beaten and brought under control.

"Does it ever go away?" I ask.

"Maybe," he hedges. "But most likely not. It is controlled and you can live for ages with it."

"Kind of like a limp then?"

More like diabetes or having red hair. He doesn't actually say that, but this is my internal processing, and I can say this without fear of victimising red-headed people. Two of my sons have red hair and are immensely ordinary and happy with it.

He decides to start the treatment right away like now. The only trouble is that they don't have the drug in stock for me to take away so they will send it to me via a courier. Fair enough. Expensive drugs through the post.

I wonder how I have acquired this disease as I do not smoke, do not drink too much, I am not massively overweight, and my diet is pretty healthy. Cancer is often linked to lifestyle – although not always. It can be a function of age, too and, given that I am a 60-year-old male, I am now in the higher risk categories for heart disease or prostate cancer, neither of which currently afflict me. Thus, I am a tad miffed about how this slow developing, unpronounceable complaint has arrived in me.

I ask Dr Al.

His scientific response is confoundingly simple; apparently, a few of my blood cells simply lost the plot.

"You are joking?"

Apparently, your blood cells are meant to die off routinely and this allows for new ones to flourish and flood my body with fresh oxygen-carrying workers. For no apparent reason, some of mine decided arbitrarily to cling on to life, presumably having too much fun. Again, I am not sure how to respond to this earth-shatteringly complex rationale.

"That's rather inconsiderate," is all I can say.

Furthermore, there is no incident that would have sparked this anti-suicidal declaration of independence.

Bugger.

I resolve to have a good rant at God about this, although I doubt whether I will receive an audible justification. This is going to be one of those 'looking back I can see…' moments. For now, I take away a mystery and will need blood tests and to see him monthly to find out how it all unfolds.

Chapter 9
October & November

I'm back in our new house after collecting our dog, Mumford, from his holiday camp at the outdoor learning centre, where I am the chairman. The teams and guests there adore him, and he has been staying there for a couple of weeks during our move.

Mumford is a nine-year-old golden retriever who is, without doubt, the most adorable, sensitive, and friendly creature that God put together. He is large and very fluffy and soft. When we got him as an eight-week-old puppy, his large feet seemed to suggest he would be a big chap, and this indeed transpired. He is more of a small lion than a large dog. His very light golden coat and polar bear features endear him to everyone he meets.

Literally everyone. When he was a puppy, cars would stop by the village green and random drivers opened their doors and asked if they could come and stroke him. He was the original Andrex puppy.

We acquired him for two reasons. Firstly, as a companion for Josh, who is in effect an only child, there being 11 years between him and Michael, and 14 between him and Nick. Secondly, because we would need to walk him a lot and this would force us to stay active.

His first night with us was traumatic. We had invested in a cage, as instructed by those in the know, and put him in it overnight. This was mistake number one! He sobbed and howled in an utterly heart wrenching way that meant I had to spend the night on the hall mat with him the other side of the child gate installed to keep him in the kitchen. This was the case the following night, too. After that, he seemed to be content enough. I mention this because, to me, Mumford is like another child and has also become a true friend who has extraordinary levels of empathy. His spiritual and emotional intelligence is remarkable.

On one walk a few months ago, we passed by the door of the hospice in our village, and he simply sat down and made to go in through the front door. He had never been in before but, in my primitive intuitive way, I reckon he knew there was sadness, pain and suffering in that building and he simply wanted to go in and lift people's spirits. I am to experience this too in special ways over the months of the illness.

The dog is also a real character in our café, welcoming everyone through the door with his joyful smile and unconditional acceptance. Adults and children alike have their spirits lifted by his warmth. To him, the café is a place of stimulus (he is clearly an extrovert) and crumbs. Cake, scones, lunches; he is essentially the world's most desirable hoover.

During October the café is open and following social distancing guidelines diligently. We are blessed to have a truly marvellous space, most of which is upstairs. Our presence on the street is a corner site on the west side of New Street in St Neots, where it joins Priory Lane, the little lane that runs to the Waitrose store, which is built on the site of the old priory itself –long since gone, of course. Our building is part of what was a former department store that was, for decades, one of the key establishments in the town until it fell victim to the evil that is online shopping.

The owner, who is now our landlord, tells us the story of how his family came to own and run the store the best part of 100 years ago, to enjoy the feast and then to endure famine so extreme that they had no choice other than to close with the loss of 30 jobs and a deep sadness. Of course, the irony is that so many local people bemoan the loss of the high street shops and communities but did little to preserve them when they could, preferring to buy things from the dark lord of Amazon for a couple of pounds less.

Our vision is opposed to this and is to create a community and place where people can come together, enjoy great company and great food, and explore creativity, all in an environment that is both stimulating and restful. Upstairs, we have our kitchen and the most marvellous of rooms in which we have our art gallery. This room is Grade 2 listed and was the original Assembly Room of St Neots, built in the 1700s.

The windows are the original ones as is the ceiling. The light is special as it floats so gracefully through the huge arched windows. Everyone who sees the space for the first time is typically amazed and awe-struck. This is thrilling for us as the project has consumed so much of us – our energy and all our money – over the time since we opened it in November 2018.

When the pandemic struck in early 2020, it was a profound disappointment as we had just begun to turn the corner into profitability and had built a strong brand from zero. We were forced to close from March through to July and then, having opened up again to the shouts of 'eat out to help out' (the chancellor's grand scheme to restart the decimated hospitality sector) in August, we were doing our best to keep our heads above water and to preserve the jobs of the 11 people connected to our project.

Although we own and run a café and art gallery business, my

main source of income, and where I spend most of my time, is a boutique consultancy that delivers leadership development solutions and coaching for executives, and runs programmes and retreats. I am often asked what I do, and when I say this, I am usually met with glazed looks. I tend to resort to saying that it's a business that runs training courses about leadership and management skills. I think that after doing this for over 20 years, my mother still has no idea what I do because it simply does not fit any proper job category that she has grown up with in her 80-plus years. I say, think teacher, only more.

The year 2020 has devastated our business. All our key clients for whom we delivered programmes in this country and all over the world have cancelled them.

Face-to-face courses are clearly not commensurate with protecting ourselves from each other and coronavirus. I spend the early part of the year working out how to stay close enough to our clients and keep them engaged and try to extract some moderate recompense for the loss of income.

By a perverse quirk of misfortune, the furlough scheme that the government has so generously introduced to keep some businesses afloat – including our café – does not apply to me as a company director. In effect, I receive precious little income for several months. I was due to travel on a dozen occasions to the Far East, the US and Europe, as had been the case in previous years, but I am literally grounded. No travel anywhere!

My airline seats are replaced by my office chair, first in the front room of our former house, and now in my new study, in which I can locate nothing having thought so carefully about where to put things. Typical. Human contact is replaced with two-dimensional video calls that take the whole world about four months to master. These are endured rather than enjoyed.

Nonetheless, in the months of April, May and June, we use the café to record some videos that we provide for our clients. A couple of my dearest friends who are actors work with me and my son Michael to produce them and we have a barrel of laughs doing it. Despite lockdowns, I am firing on many cylinders right through to the 'incident' in August and the ensuing physical shutdown in September and October.

When I post on Facebook that I have been diagnosed with this rare condition, my clients reach out to me with words of encouragement and such warmth of feeling that I am bowled over. From all around the world, I am contacted and reminded of how much I have given to people and how much of a difference I have made. I remind myself that I am not dead yet, and these words are not a eulogy, which means I am doubly humbled as they clearly must mean what they say.

I am in no state to be able to do much work. Emotionally, I am exhausted, and physically, my body is all over the proverbial place. I am not sleeping well and so do find myself having frequent naps during the day.

Part of me feels very guilty about this as it is not in my nature to do nothing, nor in my cultural upbringing, I might add.

On one such quiet morning when Caroline has gone into the café, I have a conversation with an dear old friend of mine whom I have known for close to 40 years. He is a consultant haematologist who moved from where we lived in London to Yorkshire a few years ago.

Dr Ian and I have shared many wonderful times and he was always someone that we, and many others, could call up with any number or range of medical issues, and he would delight in telling us what was wrong and what we could do about it. I have since realised that scientists and engineers alike enjoy nothing more than telling you all they know about something.

Dr Ian is bonkers, too. He once bought some new varifocal glasses and drove home in them, only to misjudge the length of his driveway and bump straight into his own house. Feeling rather stupid, he reversed and decided to reposition his car and promptly did the same thing again. I could have told him that varifocals to the uninitiated are extremely hazardous, having myself been utterly paralysed at a T-junction, unsure of how close anything really was.

This morning, he calls me to say that he has heard of my diagnosis and is concerned for me but wants to reassure me that the unpronounceable disease – WM to him and those specialists in the know – is perfectly treatable and that he has several patients with it and who are on the magic drug treatment that I am receiving. Apparently, one of his patients has returned to his full normal life as a lorry driver with no ramifications.

He asks who is treating me in Harlow. I tell him it is Dr Al (I give his full name), whereupon Dr Ian tells me that he has known Dr Al for decades and that they have worked together, shared patients (not sure how you can share a patient if I am honest) and that he is a great consultant.

Once more, I find myself bursting into tears simply because this seems to me to be another example of the details being taken care of, in my mind and in my spirit, by my God. I ask him for any advice he has for me. He says to avoid large gatherings of people because of a weakened immune system and to avoid conflicting therapies such as cocaine. Damn!

One of my clients, whom I have known for several years and have coached in a variety of roles and organisations, has taken on a very significant role in a major UK charity that has global influence. As a director of an important function, he has been building a new team around him, and he and I had agreed that we would run a workshop in person during October or November when his new team could actually meet face-to-face.

He knows about my condition and was one of the kind souls to say such lovely, reassuring things early on. We call each other and I say that I am unlikely to be able to do the two-day session in person both because I am knackered and might fall asleep mid-sentence and, more wisely, because I have been told by many folks that I should avoid contact with people because of the coronavirus. As I am desperate to be needed and not let this illness stop me completely in my tracks, I suggest that I could facilitate their strategic team building remotely using this newfangled video conferencing regime. We think it will work and I get myself psyched up for the event.

When the day comes, the client team are ensconced in a hotel in Coventry, and I am in my study. They have rigged me up to play through a large monitor in the room and they sit themselves in an orderly U-shape in front of the TV so I can see them. It would be fair to say that, while it is not the United Nations or BBC in terms of sophistication, it works, with a couple of caveats.

I can see most of the group, bar two, who are closest to me but concealed from the camera on the laptop and every time they speak, I

73

hear them loudly but have no idea who it is who is speaking. The lady at the farthest point at the head of the conference table tends to speak a lot but as she is farthest from the microphone, I pick up one word in every six.

Then, of course, there is the fact that I am talking to them in the style of Big Brother from *1984,* as my face will be about the size of a small billboard issuing instructions to them.

Remarkably, they don't seem to be intimidated, which I ascribe to the sympathy vote as I have confessed to speaking to them not quite from the side of my grave plot but encumbered with the unpronounceable illness. I am even satisfied that I have mastered the name now. Well, almost.

The event goes surprisingly well, and I feel like a superhero, having clearly performed a miracle delivering the workshop only a few weeks after being presented with the millstone of the disease. Regrettably, though, my hero's brain has failed to take account of my wimp body and, after the first of the two-hour sessions, I am exhausted and need a nap.

A lunchtime mid-workshop nap. Whoever heard of such a thing?

I shall not be confessing this lapse of professionalism to my work colleagues. I discover that talking and being totally attentive requires huge amounts of energy that I don't really have just now. The months of Covid lockdown have come at a convenient time for me as my previous high-octane years of global travel have been totally stalled this year with no trips anywhere, not even in the UK. Just as well, given that my body simply would not cope. Timing is everything, I guess.

By the end of the two days, I am chuffed to bits that the team has found it valuable and that the technology worked. Significantly, it has given me the confidence to think that I can continue to do what I love and what I do best, albeit virtually.

Over the coming months, I deliver more workshops and seminars, including one ridiculous session scheduled for five o'clock in the morning because the audience is based in the Far East. More naps are needed!

My hospital visit in late November gives me the news that my haemoglobin level has crawled up to 88. I say crawled because the original diagnosis was 75 so I guess I should be glad for the progress. This is, of course, one of those occasions when no prior knowledge is both an advantage and a disadvantage. The fact that I do not know how haemoglobin levels are either increased or decreased means I respond to Dr Al with a kind of non-plussed expression. I recall that the average is 130-140 so, in my mind, I need to be cranking things up a bit more quickly to reach those dizzy heights.

Maybe I should be eating huge steaks or drinking more red wine. Or maybe I need to reduce the red cells and increase the white ones, which presumably means eating more fish and drinking Chenin Blanc. I can but hope. The reality is that it's probably neither of these and I am going to have to trust in the power of science and medicine to work their magic on my blood cells.

Good news, Dr Al is pleased as things are going in the right direction.

"Is it fast enough?" I moot.

"Most definitely. It could be slower or have gone backwards," he tells me.

Blimey, that would be tough, I think.

He reassures me that the drugs are beginning to work.

"How long might it take for things to get back to normal?" I ask.

He won't be drawn on this. It could be months or even years.

He is pleased with the movement of the other indicators in my blood as well. In my enthusiasm to track my progress I ask for a copy of the printouts from my blood tests. Not wanting to appear a complete bozo, I look down the list of abbreviations pretending that I have the first idea of what I am reading, which, of course, I don't. He tells me that my kidneys are functioning brilliantly.

Is this important, I wonder?

Yes, because the drugs are zapping the bad cells as quickly as they can reproduce themselves and then kicking them out of my body through my kidneys. Given that I am peeing more often, I decide that this is because I have so many of the offenders to discharge. I imagine my wee becoming a fiendishly lurid colour, full of dead bodies or cells crying out: "Please don't evict us. We promise we won't do it again".

Disappointingly, everything looks pretty much the same as normal, but I still rejoice that this so basic of functions is the departure lounge itself.

Chapter 10
Christmas

Despite the forced imprisonment of Covid lockdowns during the year, the UK government, in its infinite wisdom, has, on one hand, decided to renege on an earlier promise to allow significant relaxation of restrictions over the holiday period and, on the other hand, allowed us to gather in small groups indoors with windows open (it's midwinter for goodness' sake, we are all going to die of hyperthermia in our own kitchens) and broadly within existing households or support groups. But for one day only, or maybe that includes an evening, or maybe the weekend. It's as clear as mud. Nobody has any idea what we are allowed to do.

People are floundering across the country as local restrictions are even more extreme in certain places. Some lucky citizens are allowed to go outside or, inside, or both. Others can only stay inside, but on their own, or with some family, or not. As for me, I am not sure whether I should simply straddle my front door threshold to comply. This conundrum is to prove even more farcical in a few hours' time as events unfold.

Since the 'incident' and the diagnosis, two other strange phenomena have touched my increasingly wobbly body. Firstly, I have stopped biting my nails. This might not seem like anything to write home about, but trust me, when you have been chewing your own fingertips for over 50 years, to suddenly stop doing this is very peculiar. And it happens overnight. Before the incident, I never need to use nail scissors and then I notice that I have sharp bits growing on the ends of all my fingers. We put this down to another example of how my brain is rewiring itself. Very odd indeed.

Next, my feet are swelling up. Cue a Google investigation. It seems that this can be associated with the disease.

Bother.

Now, I cannot get my slippers on without having to cut them over the instep, and I have had to rethread the laces on my shoes to accommodate my hobbit-like feet. Naturally, I am especially self-conscious about this. Having been a size nine and a half for over 50 years, I suspect I am suddenly now a couple of sizes bigger. I imagine people talking about me under their breath: "Look at that bloke trying to walk on inflated feet. It's like he has never done this before!" And it hurts.

Going for a long walk is now out of the question (if something is out of the question, what is it like if it is inside the question, I wonder?). I try this a couple of times and realise it is not nice. Moreover, I am worried that if I stand on a sharp stone that, my inflated feet will simply burst like a balloon, and I shall be sent careering off in all directions or thrust forward like a hoverboard. That would be worth watching. This prevents any reasonable exercise for a few weeks.

October brings great joy amidst the chaos of the disease. Baby Eva Richardson arrives at the end of October. She is our first grandchild. Can life get any more topsy-turvy, I wonder? Yes, as we are going to find out shortly.

According to friends who are grandparents, we are supposed to feel an overwhelming sense of love and joy for our new relative. I can only assume that this kicks in once one has made human contact rather than just seen a photo. By some miracle of the pandemic rules, we are allowed to visit her just a few days after her birth and we set off to south London to do just that.

Upon meeting her and holding her tiny being in our arms, I can see what people are on about. I am nervous, though. I am frail, tired and don't want to drop her. I have clearly forgotten how to hold a small baby, even though I have had four myself. Still, I manage some lovely moments. These are to be our only moments with her for the next few months.

We have worked out that over Christmas, we can have my 87-year-old mother with us for a few days as she has notionally been in our bubble and has been judiciously separate from all human contact for weeks. We will also have our youngest son Josh with us and hopefully, he will not bring any COVID-19 from the university. My sister and her husband could not come over, so she sent presents to us via courier. Nick and his wife Susie will appear at some point and, as for Michael and Celia, who knows when we will see them.

I drive over to Kettering to collect my mother on December 23. Moving to Godmanchester means we are 30 or so miles from her in Kettering, which is some comfort for her.

It is raining, a lot.

I mean, a serious lot.

As we reach our new house and ensconce her in the spare bedroom, it is still raining. Heavily.

The clouds are as foreboding as clouds get in England.

But it is just rain after all. What could be the problem with that? It could be two feet of snow.

At around seven in the evening, we are watching the TV and I get up to let the dog out to do his evening ablutions. Tentatively, he stares in some kind of disbelief at the road surface. It appears to be moving, flowing to be precise. This is most odd. Although we moved to be nearer to a river – in this case the Great Ouse – it is two miles away in the town and that is down a not insignificant hill.

Upon closer inspection, the flowing nature of the road is unnervingly flowing towards our house in a kind of gentle-waves-lapping-upon-the-shore motion. Maybe climate change has happened overnight, and the sea has risen 200 feet? Doubtful. We would have noticed, I guess. I pinch myself and paddle forwards in my loosened, enlarged trainers. The lapping begins to create waves around my shoes.

I lift my head.

In front of me is a field that backs onto the farm with which we share our immediate space. It is idyllic, which means we are not overlooked, other than by a family of pheasants. I realise that the water is literally pouring off the field and that the field is 100 yards wide as it abuts our little private road. Some quick mental maths later, I turn to retrieve the completely confused dog who is clearly musing that there wasn't a river here earlier. In what is best described as a mild panic, I dive inside to announce the impending crisis. I am greeted by further disbelief, and we all stand aghast at the front door. The obvious question: is this going to come into the house?

Our neighbours are oblivious to the coming end of the world so out of the kindness of my heart, I knock on their door to break the news.

We have a developing issue. A lot of water is coming off the field towards our roads and houses. And it's still raining heavily.

Crickey!

There is some good news in that it looks like the way that the paving blocks have been laid means that some of the water is being directed around the front of the houses and down the driveways between our homes and there are some drains there. For the time being, that is.

Phew!

They join me in the residential paddle, a kind of new dance involving prancing so as not to let the water into one's shoes whilst looking at one's feet and muttering in disbelief.

It is, of course, midwinter, so it is very dark and cold. Furthermore, there are no streetlights, just some quirky short poles that each have an illuminated top and are located one outside each house, presumably to demarcate the road, made of paving blocks, from areas of grass. We find it hard to evaluate the extent of the catastrophe as we stare into the darkness, searching for some primeval beast that is about to emerge from the farm buildings.

What we need is a little blitz spirit. We are being invaded and we need to rebut it. Cue Dad's Army – literally an army of dads, sons, and mums.

For a moment or two, I consider adopting the role of Captain Mainwaring, but this is assumed by my neighbour who bears an uncanny resemblance to Arthur Lowe and who relishes the challenge. I end up blending Sergeant Wilson seamlessly with Corporal Jones, merging my effortless natural charm and 'would you mind awfully' sense of things will simply be fine, with a rapidly accelerating sense of panic as I rush around randomly. This is indeed a time to panic, Mr

Mainwaring. I am chuffed though, that I have banished any channelling of Fraser and his trademark 'we're all doomed.'

I open the garage to see what we have got in there that could possibly help hold back the tide. Boxes of files perhaps might work, but they would simply get soaked and disintegrate. Some suitcases, perhaps? But they are empty and would float away, and they are in the loft anyway. Speed is going to be important and getting into the loft without a loft ladder could take up precious defensive time. Perhaps the inflatable boat. Yes, of course. But where the hell is that and it will take some blowing up. Damn, where is the pump?

I have no idea.

Ah, the tent. Might that work?

Better still, two rolled-up old carpets.

Brilliant. We could wrap them in the groundsheet and behold, flood defence.

At this point, Caroline points out that we do have some flood barriers.

You are joking, surely? Who has actual flood barriers and what form could they take?

Apparently, because our café in St Neots is officially in a flood risk area, we are obliged to have some kind of inflatable sandbag type things that we can put up against the doors to stop water from getting in.

Excellent, but they are in St Neots, which is 20 minutes away. Without a second thought, she leaps into the van and speeds off to get them. I warn her not to be too shocked if, upon her return, we are all swept away.

I decide to call my son Nick, who lives 20 minutes away in Cambridge, to explain how we could do with his muscle to help with the resistance effort. My other son, Josh, is now fully awake to the crisis and paddling in his flip-flops like a 1970s hippy at a waterlogged Glastonbury as he heads off towards the advancing wall of mud and water. His laughter and glee at the adventure seem vaguely incongruent with the possibility of a wrecked new house. But hey, he seems to be enjoying himself as he proceeds armed only with a shovel and optimism.

He starts to dig a trench to try to divert the flood. He is joined by Nick, who has arrived with tales of dramatic floods on the roads from Cambridge that he simply ploughed through, driven by his desire to rescue his ailing father and mother. He loves a challenge and sets about the war effort with extraordinary vigour. The rolled-up carpet is covered with a plastic groundsheet and laid in the torrent to divert the rush of water to the side of the house.

At this point, I remember my aged mother, who has been told to stay in the lounge and not to worry. She has been joined by the dog, who has clearly decided that this whole thing is way too stressful, even for his natural curiosity. Mind you; perhaps it's the driving rain and freezing temperature that has persuaded him that it is best to stay in the warm. Or maybe he has an unbowed confidence in his humans to sort this out. I doubt it, but who knows?

My mother is remarkably unphased for someone who cannot swim (seriously, she cannot) and could be faced with a tsunami sooner than she thinks. But then, I am not sure what help she would be other than to tell us stories of going through the last war. I check she is OK and reassure her that we have a plan. If only…

Caroline returns with the flood defences. These amount to long sausages filled with material that expands when laid out and wet. Apparently, we must soak them first in the sink.

You cannot be serious!

The irony is not lost on us as we stare at the gentle flood. We decide to plop them in it anyway and they had better jolly well expand in situ in front of the door.

By now, Nick and Josh are shovelling with abandon and have regressed to 10-year-olds on a beach channelling the sea around a sandcastle. Only this castle is our actual castle. The locals have come out in significant numbers and, armed with spoons, spades, and anything else that might shift the earth, are building levees.

I realise that my feet are freezing cold and sodden as I have been paddling around in my trainers. I am also reminded that I am technically very ill and, while the drugs are beginning to have a positive impact, I am ordered to come in and warm up. Wise, I suspect. Josh, too, realises that his feet are freezing in his flip-flops and dons my wellies to go straight back out on the front line again.

The unrelenting rain is now flowing ceremoniously across the paving and being channelled towards the driveways between houses. The drains are completely useless to the extent that after about 30 minutes or so, Captain Mainwaring's driveway is two feet under water that is rushing into his garage and building up rather like a freshly dammed reservoir.

As such a reservoir is not on the estate plans, Nick acts as a dam buster pilot and smashes the base of our fence to release the water on the drive. This does the trick. The torrent smashes into our garden and down into the garden of the house behind ours, helpfully a good two or three feet below ours. Helpfully for us, that is.

On the other side of the garden, and to stop water rushing into our garage, the diversions have created an emerging lake that needs emptying quickly. Cue yet another trench, quickly dug out of the fresh turf, to carry the river down the incline to the rear neighbours' gardens. Our garden is beginning to resemble the Nile Delta. Mind you, that's nothing compared to the inland sea developing in the gardens behind us.

Foolishly, the boys lift a fence panel and I, now clad in wellies myself, step into their garden and promptly into two feet of water. The boys then decide to lower the panel and leave me there so that they can go around the roads to inspect the carnage. Paddling has now become fully-fledged wading, in the dark, in a stranger's garden. I was expecting to see them at their back door, but there is no sign of them. Do they not realise that the water is lapping at their French windows? I tap gently on the window as I realise that it could be a tad unsettling to find a bedraggled old bloke wading through your garden whose only justification for being there is that he came through the fence.

But it is to no avail. There is no response. This is very odd.

I look for an exit lest I be overwhelmed by the flood. I do not want to be the subject of this year's weirdest headline: 'Old man dies not of blood cancer but of drowning, having got lost in his neighbour's garden on a cold winter's night.' The only viable exit is via their side gate, which I can open like a lock gate against the force of the water.

I hear voices. As I round the corner, there are my sons and wife talking with the owners at their side door explaining that they have some portable flood defences to share if they would like them. I appear from the shadows.

The owners turn and look perplexed as I wade out of their garden. I decide to play it cool and simply walk on past saying that they might want to look at the increasing amount of water creating a new manmade lake in Cambridgeshire. They decline the flood barriers. The next-door house does not, as their garden is also filling up quickly and they only moved in today. Wow, that's quite a welcome.

During these scenes, my mother has been vaguely oblivious to the catastrophe, which is probably a good thing. I pop back and fill her in and say that I am phoning the emergency number in the 'welcome to your new house pack.' Surprisingly, it does not have a section entitled 'What to do if your home is surrounded by a moat.'

This brings out the site manager who joins in the digging of trenches with the assembled locals. Only, he has a digger.

That night, two large lorries pump gallons of water from the estate and, as we have managed successfully to divert the water around our houses in the form of some splendid new Hapsburg Palace-esque water garden (Vienna has some fabulous water gardens, I am told), we crash to sleep at some unearthly hour. The lapping of water and gently flowing streams give us some strange dreams.

The morning heralds a new landmark. A sizeable dyke that runs for a good 50 metres across the front of our little close. The digger seems to have dug this out. Hurrah and phew. But…

As Christmas Day proceeds, the dyke is filling with water very quickly and, contrary to physics, it is not flowing away towards the natural ditch that it is joined to further along the road. This brings out Messrs Mainwaring, Wilson, Jones, Fraser and all and sundry to inspect this remarkable phenomenon. Worryingly, there is also a lake forming directly in front of our house and the dyke's sides – levees basically – are only just holding.

The collective wisdom is that this is now a lake some four-feet deep and, were the levees to be breeched, this would not go well for us. Furthermore, we deduce that the genius who dug the ditch simply forgot to put any kind of gradient in it and, as a result, it flows nowhere.

We muse about setting up our own off-grid hydroelectric power station, but instead, having found my role as Sergeant Wilson very much to my liking, I decide to calm things down and call the site manager again and ask him to remedy the situation.

Okay, I might have uttered words like 'your reputation is going to be trashed when this hits the Press unless you come and fix this today', but my overall tone of dangerously cross but basically civilised new homeowner persuades him to leave his family on Boxing Day, to garner the support of his digger driver (the numpty who did it wrong in the first place, perhaps) and to have another go. This time, bribed with a bottle of wine each from my rack, they proceed to channel out an even longer dyke back towards the unoccupied house next door and beyond into their site itself. It works as the level recedes over the coming days, presumably rendering their site rather quaggy.

Two even larger banks of earth begin to appear as the digger continues its work, creating a barrier. We can all sleep assured in the knowledge that digger bloke has got it under control. Can't we?

Chapter 11
Boxing Day

On Boxing Day, we receive a flood warning for St Neots, the town in which our café is located. There is a likely risk of flooding to the High Street, so we should take measures. Can this year get any more ridiculous? Well, yes.

St Neots High Street has flooded once in 100 years, I think, so this is either a massive piece of sensationalism on the part of the environment agency, or we should go and check. I decide that my health is up to it, just, so I volunteer to go and see what might be happening while Caroline does other things and aims to join me shortly. Then, together, we can work out if we need to do anything.

The drive there follows the river for a while and that allows me to catch sight of the beautiful spectacle of the Ouse flexing its muscles as it pours into all the surrounding fields around the ancient town of Godmanchester. The Romans built a town here – Durovigutum – at the point where the river was presumably fordable as Ermine Street headed north from Londinium.

This is the River Great Ouse (not the lesser River Ouse, in Yorkshire, you understand). Ouse is an ancient English word meaning 'water' – not very imaginative, is it?

Rather like 'avon' means river. So, the River Great Ouse simply means rather a lot of water, which is precisely what we have now. It is a majestic river that meanders gently and widely from the English Midlands northwards to meet the sea in The Wash.

Normally, it is tranquil; the type of quintessential English river that would have been used to float oaks to the ship-building yards at Kings Lynn. Today though, it has formed vast lakes in the flooded meadows and is in danger of breaching the defences in Godmanchester itself.

Arriving in St Neots, the River Great Ouse has not yet flooded Market Square and High Street, but it has flooded waterside pubs and parks, creating islands of litter bins that are now more like buoys in the ocean. If it carries on like this, things could get grim. Crowds have been drawn to the town to witness the power of nature despite the guidance that we are all supposed to be staying home in some kind of lockdown because of the pandemic. I guess rules don't apply when faced with a once-in-a-century flood.

Even though the water has not reached the café, I enter in and decide that caution is the best approach. I had better move some furniture up on to tables and clear lowly positioned cups and paraphernalia from the counter. It seems logical and, that way, we will have done our best to limit damage. All our sockets are a couple of feet above floor level for precisely this possibility. I lift some chairs a little and shuffle them around a bit. I decide to lift one on to a table and take up the advised position to lift with a straight back and bent legs. See, I know this stuff.

Bugger.

I have completely overlooked the fact that my muscles have all but vanished over the past three months. More accurately, my brain – which you will recall has been losing connection with my limbs on numerous occasions – still sees chair, table and simply says, 'go for it.' Easy-peasy, lemon-squeezy. My body, on the other hand, is faced with a dilemma. It desperately wants me to succeed and boost my flagging confidence, but I know this is not going to be possible as the simple laws of physics will require me to be a featherweight weightlifter rather than simply, well, er, a featherweight!

But, between them, my brain and my body hatch a plan; I will lift this chair onto the table using those muscles that I do have, not located in my arms and legs, but still flapping around my midriff. Genius. In a nanosecond of decisiveness, I lift the chair onto the table and simultaneously yelp as pain arrives in my lower back.

Bugger.

When doctors ask you to describe pain, they often use phrases like 'stabbing pain,' which I always think is ridiculous because I have never been stabbed in my back, so I wouldn't know. Maybe it's an ache. You're kidding, of course. This hurts like hell. I resolve to tell the doctor that it is as if I have been shot in my back because I have never been shot either and neither will he have been, I guess. But between us, we can agree this is bad.

I freeze in a contorted pose, rather like a Picasso Cubist Period painting, a position so bizarre as to be beyond description. Movement suddenly seems like a bonkers idea. My brain has now woken from its semiretirement to take control. The pain receptors are going into overdrive and overriding everything that my brilliant, logical and analytical brain is suggesting.

Get to one of the sofas and sit down.

But that will mean moving and will, in all probability, trap the nerve or whatever has happened again. So, don't.

But I must. I can't stand here like a surreal Dali statue. Caroline will wonder what is going on – living art perhaps.

You have been warned.

Ok I'll take the risk.

I grit my teeth and tense my jaw (odd, that always helps, doesn't it?) and, grope the back of a chair and shuffle to the sofa, letting myself down cautiously into its welcome embrace.

Something has gone awry, I deduce.

My over-ambitious attempt to prevent flood damage has resulted in me potentially being the first human victim of flooding in St Neots, ever. It occurs to me that, unless Caroline arrives to rescue me, I might simply be overwhelmed by rising flood waters and drown, fully awake on my own sofa but unable to move off it. Then, I come to my senses and realise that I could float with the rising waters and perhaps come to rest on the countertop next to the coffee machine. That would be nice.

I have 'put my back out' (such an odd phrase, really) before and it takes a while to 'come back in.' This is not what I need right now, though. I resolve to tough it out and pretend it isn't that bad.

Caroline arrives to find me sitting on an upright chair, which was quite an achievement to reach, and I tell her that I have 'tweaked something in my back.' I tend to think that tweaking is such a gentle verb and implies a minor inconvenience. Would that this were the case.

Between us, we lift some more things up. I am careful not to show my contorted grimace too much, but I do make lots of in-pain noises so that it is clear something is awry. I get a modicum of sympathy laced with oodles of 'What on earth were you thinking? You're ill, for goodness' sake.'

As we head back to our house, I sense that this minor tweaking might not be so minor, but I hope that it is only a moderate rather than a major inconvenience. Equally, we cross our fingers that the rising flood waters do not reach the once-in-a-century level and flood the High Street and our little café.

We have been forced to close the café again because of the pandemic after being allowed to open a bit in early December. We have no idea how long it will now have to remain shut. The general consensus is that the government has made complete Horlicks of the rules, guidelines or whatever we want to call them, such that nobody is quite sure whether they can leave their homes or not, on which days, and which way they should turn if they do.

Moreover, we are not sure whether we can meet anyone we know or don't know, or whether we should simply pretend any actual meeting is a complete accident lest we are stopped by some newly formed secret police who have monitored that we have left our house twice in a day.

It is quite clear that the citizens of St Neots have ignored these guidelines by and large as they gather in large numbers to check out the flood in the town. Typical, when we want large numbers of people to come into the town, we are not able to serve them any coffee.

Over the coming days, everyone holds their breath as the waters rise and fall, without breaching the defences into the town centre itself. Quite frankly, to do so would mean a rise of some 30 feet or so on the bank opposite the flooded meadows and if that happened, goodness knows what it would mean. We all let out a collective 'phew,' although, for a good number of people whose homes are on the river flood plains, their Christmas is ruined. It is a bit odd that many of the homes that one might expect to get flooded actually do, and they do not make the papers, whereas our new homes, threatened by run-off from a field, make the local rag. All we had was a ruined garden and some damage in the garages. We count ourselves lucky.

Chapter 12
January 2021

The new year brings a fresh challenge for me. Just when I think I am managing to make some progress on the blood front, my sheer stupidity – or should I say my well-intentioned but slight over-confidence in my ability – renders me useless, again! How much more of this male emasculation can a man take? To put it bluntly, my back has not just been 'put out a bit,' it has surrendered to a totally humiliating defeat and the mild tweak has morphed into complete immobility.

This time, it's not just a case of my muscles forgetting what to do; it's a case of my brain now overriding any movement because the sharp stabbing or shooting, or the 'being hit in the back by a spear,' pain in my back will be too great. I arrived at utterly patheticville and duly checked in at Feeble Manor Hotel. I can barely move. I cannot get out of bed or even lie down comfortably. As for turning over, this requires so much effort as to prove pointless.

I decide that I must sleep in a spare bed again, not because I am melting (thankfully, that has finished), but because that mattress is a futon and provides me with some support to manoeuvre myself up. Our marriage bed is large, warm, and built for cuddles and slow mornings.

As I must raise myself up using only my arms supported by facial contortions, I am forced to push down into the bed and it, unhelpfully, offers no resistance at all. It is rather like trying to push off from a vat of jelly.

I reckon that the Japanese know a thing or two about bad backs as they have futon mattresses, which are just one degree of comfort up from sleeping on a car park. We're talking firm. We're talking about giving me some good support. Now, I am not sure what is in the futon mattress, but it sure isn't feathers. I sense it is more like builders' putty that just gives a tiny bit and needs some serious manipulation to warm it up first.

Once I have made it to the bed, eventually, and after much shrieking and groaning, and with the help of my walking sticks (how prescient was Caroline in buying these from a charity shop a few months before), I lie prone on my back on the unmoulded surface and try and get some sleep. During the night, the putty moulds itself to my contorted shape, presumably to help me.

Sadly, the effect is the opposite. I have actually created a sculptor's mould of myself in the futon mattress and when I try and turn over to the other side, I have to raise myself out of the mould and over the side walls to create a new impression.

My bladder has still not reset itself to normal adult operating mode. I still need to go to the toilet in the night. More than once.

Bugger.

At least the now malleable mattress allows me to move ever so slowly onto my side such that I can use my arm, still a tad enfeebled, to push myself up into a sitting position with my feet on the floor. I reach for the stick and clasp it with both my hands, count to 10 and raise myself up with all the strength I have left in me, pushing down onto the stick to get my leg muscles to at least try to lift my frame that is now at least two stones lighter than it used to be.

The effort is fabulously draining. I shuffle to the bathroom and perform whilst holding myself up with one hand on the stick. I simply don't trust my back to support me.

I always have the stick with me, even in the shower, after discovering that it is not possible to put a chair in there safely. I am in a state of permanent exhaustion due to the sheer effort of moving anywhere without whatever it is that is trapped in my back, pinching the nerves with such alacrity that I collapse.

This goes on for a couple of weeks until the next incident.

It is Sunday morning and I am lying on a hospital bed in Hinchingbrooke Hospital while I have an ECG and further tests, this time on my heart. I have been sent here by the paramedics who were called to my house by my wife because I am, it seems, having some major palpitations. To be honest, I was fine but then sitting in a chair in the lounge I suddenly felt as if my heart was going to erupt through my head as a thumping beat became so loud and irregular in my body.

It was like a terrible disco where the drum and bass has got out of control. This spooked me to such an extent that I panicked (again!) and Caroline dialled 111. The conversation was protracted and very strange as I tried to explain to the guy what was going on. He called a local doctor, who then called us and said they were sending an ambulance.

Ah. That does not sound good.

The paramedics arrive and after some crazy but necessary shenanigans around opening all the windows and doors because of COVID-19, they perform a local ECG on me. This reveals some irregularities, such that the lead team member invites Caroline to 'pack me a bag.'

"Why? Am I going somewhere?" I ask.

"You are going to hospital because your heart is missing some beats on a very irregular basis."

"Is this anything to do with my overall condition, which is basically wrecked?"

"Could be."

Due to my back issues, I need to be helped into the ambulance and, as lying down takes a while, they get me onto a wheely bed contraption to do it. Priceless. So, not only have I had to use a wheely push walker thingy, now I am being slid into an ambulance. It's been over 50 years since I was last in an ambulance, so I am not at all at ease with this. But they reassure me that it is a new version with lots of bells and whistles, although they tell me that there are some aspects about it that are less than perfect.

Do I care? Nope. That's because, right now, I am on my own again, and feeling very vulnerable. Am I having a heart attack? Will this get me instead of the lymphoma?

Mercifully, my heart palpitations seem to have slowed and I don't feel like I am going to explode, which is helping me relax. In addition to Covid meaning that I am not allowed to be accompanied when we arrive at the appropriate entrance, I am told I must be placed in an isolation ward bed.

"What on earth for? It's not like I have Ebola, or do I?"

"No," I'm told. "Your wife said that you had a recent recurrence of the shingles you had a couple of years ago, and, because a nurse in the hospital has not had chickenpox, we need to put you out of the way so you cannot contaminate her."

"Are you serious? A nurse in the hospital is anxious about contacting chicken pox. From me." "Better to be safe than sorry." Marvellous.

I find myself in a characterless room on my own and propped up on one of those gloriously uncomfortable hospital beds that have rails along the sides to stop me from falling off. My back is giving me considerable jip, as they say, and I cannot find a position that is restful at all. I am fidgeting. A male nurse arrives to find out what is going on. He is from Portugal and is a joyful character. We decide we need another ECG and blood test.

"The results of the ECG are fine," he says.

"What do you mean?"

"Normal and no sign of irregularities."

"Seriously?"

"Seems so."

"So, how come it wasn't before?"

"No idea. But these things do happen. Best that you came in to be checked over. The good news though is that your haemoglobin is up to over 90 which is good progress if you were down at 78 a short while ago."

That's encouraging.

"So, what do we do now?" I ask.

"Well, it's probably best that you rest for a while in here and we can do an ECG again in a while to make sure that things have stabilised. Then the doctor will have to agree you can leave."

I settle down with a book. Caroline has packed me an

overnight bag, as instructed, although it feels large enough and heavy enough for a fortnight's stay. It remains on the floor as I cannot lift it. I guess the paramedics must have brought it in.

In a little while I need the loo. Given that I am in an isolation ward when I ask where the toilet is, I am told I cannot leave the room. Who knew that chicken pox was so infectious just from wandering around to get to the toilet?

Presented with a cardboard receptacle in which to pee, I freeze momentarily. Anyone who has ever had to perform into such a device must surely have experienced the same kind of sudden panic. What if I cannot manage it? What if it gushes over the sides? What if the cardboard is faulty and simply dissolves in my hands? Perhaps that has happened before, and what a shock that must have been. Reassuringly, nothing untoward occurs.

Some time later, a second normal ECG suggests that this whole thing has been a dream. But a few hours ago, my heart was pounding out of my head. What is going on?

All I know is that I have been enquiring of God about this, and, thus far, silence. Nonetheless, I am massively relieved when the doctor tells me that I can go home now, and he prescribes me some powerful painkillers for my back that are only available in hospital packaging because they're that strong. I call Caroline and tell her that I will meet her at the front door.

I discover that I still cannot lift my overnight bag. As nobody wants to be near me in the corridor, lest the pox leaps at them, I cannot expect anyone to come to my rescue. There's only one thing for it. I simply kick the bag along the corridor, giving the floor a good clean as I go. It's a surreal sight, for sure.

A guy with a stick, clearly in some discomfort, shuffling along the corridor and kicking a black holdall as he goes. He's clearly a lost vagrant. I greet people as I pass them: nurses completing forms, doctors checking diagnoses, porters moving things. They observe me in a state of disbelief, smile and carry on with whatever they are doing. Perhaps I am not really there because I am left to keep kicking and shuffling all the way to the front door, where Caroline eventually picks me up.

Well, that was an interesting way to spend a Sunday, I exclaim. I thought I was dying (again), only to be proved very much alive and kicking (still, mercifully). It seems like I am being taken to the edge of my comfort zone and then way beyond it into a zone filled with fog through which I have no way of finding a route on my own. I am having to trust others and God like never before. My own sense of natural strength and capability counts for very little just now. I soon discover that this does not improve over the coming few months.

On the day of my January appointment with Dr Al, I am stuck in bed. Quite literally. I find that, despite moving to the spare room to sleep on the futon, it does not seem to be helping, as the trapped nerves in my back are preventing me from lifting my back off the mattress unless I can get myself into a position from which I can use my still pathetically wasted arms to force myself up. This whole procedure can take many minutes and is beyond me on several occasions. I have had to resort to peeing in the night into a Tupperware measuring jug that Caroline has kindly provided me with. I confess to some depressive thoughts about this.

Surely, this is the kind of thing that only very old people have to do, not someone who is just turned 60 and was playing cricket only a year or so ago.

Today, though, I must get up and find a way to travel the 50 miles to the hospital to have my blood test. It is only four months since the diagnosis and there is a long way to go, I keep being told.

No joy.

No way this is going to happen.

Caroline calls Nick and asks him to come over, which he graciously does. He is working from home, as everyone is these days because of the pandemic.

The two of them stare at me like some engineering challenge – they both have mathematical and engineering problem-solving brains. I lie there with an air of utter defeatism. Every time I try to move, the pain is extreme, and my brain simply overrides everything. Mumford is present at the other side of the bed with his front legs on the bed itself, reaching out to me. His distress is palpable and deeply moving.

The two engineers would erect an A-frame over the bed and hoist me up like an engine being extract from an old Ford Anglia if they could. The next best option is a large sheet. Picture, if you can, those wonderful documentaries showing whales being moved from one part of the world to another, when they are hoisted in a harness, put into a crate full of water and flown thousands of miles to their new home.

The sheet is carefully passed under my body and Nick then collects the two ends and simply pulls them so that I rise, ever so slowly, a bit like Darth Vader, to a sitting position and then to a standing pose. The pain is still there, of course, but as I am not using any of my own muscles or strength, this seems to work. I let out a hiss of relief, not unlike Darth Vader's. Of disbelief.

One problem, though, is that we are now out of time. Getting me into the car and being driven there, and getting out the other end is clearly going to be a joke. Ever resourceful, Caroline has a plan. We call the hospital and say, we cannot make it, but we are going to see if we can send the blood test results from the test at Hinchingbrooke last Sunday to Dr Al so he can see for himself that there has been some progress on the bloods front at least.

NHS staff may be under pressure, but they continue to pull out the stops against all odds. Through the miracle of email and the NHS systems, he receives these results which he finds encouraging. Well at least something is going according to plan. I commit to doing my very best to being able to get to the February appointment and, if I give myself a couple of weeks' head start, I should be able to make it up, get dressed and downstairs to the car in time.

This cannot continue. We must get you to a chiropractor. That would be good.

Through a local contact, we find one not too far away. Reassuringly, we discover that she specialises in horses and dogs. Yes really. Physio for horses and dogs, and the occasional old bloke.

Are we sure about this?

Well, she might have a big hoist I could use, or some powerful horse tranquilisers, although I think those are technically a banned drug for humans on the basis that they can kill us quite easily.

Upon arrival at her equine and human treatment centre – not a sign you see too often, let's be honest – I shuffle gingerly into the place to be greeted by a tall middle-aged woman standing in front of a wall covered in rosettes. Ah, she is clearly a horsey person. I want to ask her so many questions about the technicalities of physiotherapy on horses and dogs, but my mind is so focused on not making a complete arse of myself, so I decide to park those for a later date. Unfortunately, I fail.

Caroline is invited to sit outside – she's getting used to this – and I am ushered into the treatment room. I notice an absence of straw on the floor, so I deduce that this is not where she brings the horses, much to my relief. In fact, the room is remarkably spartan, with just a tiny table and chair in the corner and another chair on which I am asked to sit. There is also a padded plank. She doesn't appear to go for the whole ambient music and scent thing that I was expecting, or rather hoping for. My experiences of massages in hotels around the world are basically of pampered luxury. This has the impending sense of, shall we say, functional discomfort. I am not disappointed.

After a lengthy interrogation about my condition, and the tall story about how I end up being so immobile (she doesn't quite laugh at the flood and putting my back out episode, but I can tell she is a tad bemused about how someone who appears intelligent can have got himself into such a state), I am invited to approach the plank and lie on it, face down. By plank, I mean a therapy bench-cum-table that is barely 18 inches wide and seems to have no obvious signs of comfort other than some shiny padding. Clearly, horses and dogs don't mind the basic approach.

I'm not good at moving and lying down, but I will do my best.

"Don't rush. Take your time," she says.

I do.

Once on my front and with my face in the convenient gap, she moves my legs and checks if they are of equal length. All good, then.

"Can you turn on to your front, please?"

"No. Not easily."

"Take your time."

"But I cannot get up from this position. I will need to roll onto my side first."

"That's fine. Do that."

I begin the process and realise that the plank is far too narrow for this manoeuvre. I warn her that I am likely to roll onto the floor and then we are both doomed.

"Oh dear. What might help?"

"Could you provide some kind of support for me

as I roll a bit?"

"How about we put the chair alongside you, and you can use that."

Given the absence of any other items of furniture, that'll have to do. A combination of the chair, her arms, and some fabulously loud exhalations on my part, eventually, I am on my back, precariously teetering on the edge of the plank.

"You'll need to move over so you are fully on the bench."

"I can see why that would be helpful, but let me tell you how tricky that is for me."

"Do your best."

I did and, eventually, I arrive at the ideal resting place. She lifts my legs in turn and feels around my pelvis and prods here and there, apparently to check that there is nothing more seriously wrong. Then, the fun begins.

"Ok, so let's sit up and see if we can find a position for you to be comfortable so that we can feel the discs."

"But I can't sit up."

"Seriously?"

"Yes. This is part of the problem. It hurts too much."

"Can I help you then? I will support you."

"We can try."

She puts her arms around me under my shoulders and lifts me, too quickly. I let out the most inappropriately loud cry of pain – like a child-birthing noise, but louder. She is shocked but continues to lift me to the seated position. I am crying in pain as I eventually find myself standing on one side of the bench, bent over with my arms on the bench in a pose that resembles the waiting to be caned in the headmaster's study pose (not that I ever had to do that, you understand!). I do not know how I ended up in this position, but it is about the only pose I can rest in without trapping the nerves.

"Let's not do that again," she decides.

"Let's not," I agree.

"Can you get to a seated position on the bench?"

"Maybe. I'll try."

It takes about 20 minutes in total for me to shift from the lying down to a seated pose. Sloths have been known to move quicker than this. Goodness knows what this must sound like to Caroline who is outside the room. Panting like I've just been 10 rounds with Anthony Joshua and supporting myself with my hands on my thighs, I am sitting as she proceeds to use some kind of staple gun on my back.

Apparently, she needs to shock my connections back into their normal state such that my brain recognises the discs in my back and presumably overrides the pain from the trapped nerves. Once stapled, I am to be lasered.

No warm ylang ylang oil for me. But a horse laser, perhaps.

"Let me know if it gets too hot," she says.

I muse for a moment on how the horses or dogs let her know when it gets a tad hot, but I decide not to raise this with her as I am focusing on not collapsing on to the ground and causing myself even more embarrassment.

The laser is, apparently, the newest form of massage treatment, and it presumably means she avoids having to use her hands and fists so much. It is certainly pleasantly warm. In a moment of profound common sense, she says she will do these treatments in a sitting position in the future and skip the lying down bits.

"I think our goal is to simply get you moving," she adds. "Walking without the aid of the stick because your posture is all over the place." You don't say!

An hour or so after entering her room gingerly with my stick, I shuffle out and proceed to walk a few paces without relying on the stick for psychological and physical support. I wonder if I could have a rosette for my human dressage routine. In the car, I am exhausted and not sure whether to feel encouraged or depressed. This is going to take a while she had told me. The combination of weak muscles and a psychological and physical blockage means I am in a poor state.

January, February, and March pass with us in lockdown as a nation and with me imprisoned in my house, struggling up and down stairs. I make a further few visits to the chiropractor to be stapled and lasered some more, and it does improve my movements, little by little.

I can still barely reach down to put my socks on or do up my shoes even when in a seated position. People tell me that chronic back issues can take ages to remedy themselves. I guess that when I add this to my shocked body in all its confusion, I shouldn't be surprised that I am making such slow progress.

It is torment. All my life, I have been someone who constantly moves forward and juggles lots of ideas and projects. I hate inertia. Recently, some of my old school friends retired from their careers and have begun to settle into the third phase of their lives, according to the accepted plans. You know, the kind of thing. Retire with a large pension that allows you to travel a lot, buy a second home somewhere nice, play with some new projects, and generally take it slow.

As I enter my seventh decade and my third phase, I do not have a large pension to draw upon because I have never settled into one career role long enough. I do not have a second home, although I would have liked one, I am sure. France was always our preferred location. But I do have lots of projects on the go. The biggest by far, and all-consuming, is the café.

When we began the project in 2018, we thought we would be committing some funds to it and would investing our time and energy to build something that we believed demonstrated how people could connect better in person and tap into innate creativity thereby releasing joy, warmth and the best aspects of humanity. We wanted to model an ethical and sustainable business that traded responsibly and employed people fairly.

The first year was hard for sure as we lost lots more money and, of course, it takes time to build a brand and a reputation. Nonetheless, midway through the second year, we were beginning to make good strides as sales volumes were up, workshops were being run, and people loved our funky and quirky space.

Then, the pandemic hit… And fear grips people.

We are told to shut down. Then we are allowed to open. Then, we are told to close again. Then we are allowed to open for takeaway only. We negotiate some grants from the government and, loans from the bank, and a reduction in our rent with our landlord.

The government's scheme to pay employees 80% of their wages during the pandemic allows us to keep our staff team with us for now. Mind you, the uncertainty of these days for our fledgling business is stressful for sure. How will we emerge, if indeed we do at all?

Caroline and I do not take any income from the café project. Quite the opposite, in fact. We have been propping it up with loans and investments since inception, tens of thousands of pounds worth. It's our choice, though.

Over the recent years, I have been blessed to be able to earn a good salary as a director of a consultancy business delivering learning programmes focused on leadership development and executive coaching. This has been enough for us to live on and, as we have now moved house, we are saving on transport costs, as everyone is during the pandemic, and mortgage costs. That is until now.

For reasons best known only to the chancellor, who, by the way, is seriously rich in his own right, company directors cannot get access to handouts from the furlough schemes. So, for the best part of the year, we have no real income as a family. I can work from home in small stints, but our clients have been slow to take up any kind of learning initiative. To be more precise, they have all pretty much stalled and shut themselves down, preferring only to have their people do proper work and be on call all the time from their homes, their bedrooms, and their kitchens.

One thing for sure about this pandemic is that it will change the ways people perform their work in quite a dramatic fashion. Offices become ghost ships. Large city centres are empty of people.

As for my strengths of being with people in person, goodness knows how, if at all, this will unfold over the coming months. One client is keen to start a key leadership programme that we have been asked to deliver for them.

Beginning in May, we decide to do this entirely over Zoom, along with other programmes and workshops for some other clients. My heart sinks at the prospect of spending days on end in front of my computer screen, but it does at least mean that, from spring onwards, I can earn some money and be able to feel of some value instead of a pathetic creature. My relief is huge.

What I find curious though, is that, when people see me on the video conferencing screens, they all say how well I look. I thank them, of course, but then I ask them to be honest and not just humour me.

Honestly, they say, you look great.

I find this odd, but I presume I must have looked like a walking ghost a few months ago. Fortunately, none of them can see me moving rather slowly and gingerly around as my back and muscles try to remember what the hell they are supposed to be doing.

I am encouraged.

My monthly visits to the hospital and Dr Al reveal that the drug is working. Hallelujah! My haemoglobin count is increasing and is now above 100, just. The trajectory is positive. Phew. Had I been on some chemotherapy blunderbuss of a treatment, my hair might have fallen out and I might have needed steroids and the like. Each month, I might have had to take two weeks out to receive and then recover from the poison entering my body to try to slaughter the disease.

As a child, I remember a neighbour's daughter being treated for leukaemia as a 10-year-old and all her hair falling out. In the late 1960s and early 1970s, none of us knew much about that kind of thing, and she became a local curiosity in the streets and in schools. Sadly, I cannot recall if she survived or not and, I confess that I am ashamed about this.

And here I am, feeling better and apparently looking fabulous. What miracle is this!

Nonetheless, these early months of 2021 are prompting so many questions about our material future alongside those obvious questions about my physically healthy future, or not.

Chapter 13
A Year On

I have been encouraged to tell this story for several reasons. Primarily, my family and others have been amused by and, in some cases, actually laughed out loud as I have described moments along the journey. They felt that others would do likewise. Who can say? Secondly, and quite naturally, writing these things down is a cathartic experience.

As I write and reflect on the bizarre events of this year, I find myself laughing too at times, whilst at other times I experience joy, perhaps amazement or bemusement, sometimes gratitude, then sadness.

Additionally, as I have been writing, I wonder if there are things that I can distil from the experiences and – please forgive me for the mild arrogance – even share with others. Maybe.

Folk have asked me over this journey whether it has changed my life in any way. I know what they are getting at. Of course, it has. How could it not?

One year after the initial episodes, as I write this in October 2021, I am doing well physically. I have been visiting the hospital each month for blood tests and a consultation with Dr Al, with encouraging results.

In the early summer, I sit in the comfy chairs of the cancer unit and present my arm for a sample to be extracted. These days, I bleed like a normal, generous soul. No more do I have to be warmed up with the electric blanket. To be honest, I feel something of a fraud because, well, I feel fine.

Evidently, many of the individuals who join me in the cancer unit on Friday morning are not feeling fine. I wonder what they think when they look at me showing up for a cup of tea and a biscuit in exchange for a couple of vials of blood, clearly looking in rude health. I try to hide my embarrassment internally. I smile as I make eye contact and ask how they are doing. I am not sure if this is appropriate or not, but as I hear the nurses asking this, I figure that it is OK.

The nurses enquire the same of me, to which I sheepishly reply, fine, actually. Everyone is happy to say exactly how they are doing:

"I've had a rough couple of weeks."

"I'm doing much better now."

"I'm still feeling tired."

"They're not sure if it has spread."

This last one shatters me. How do you respond to someone who you can tell is unwell because they look grim, and they themselves know something is not good? Life doesn't prepare you for this kind of interaction. And yet, I know a tiny bit of their state. A few months ago, I felt grim and looked it too. I have been spared the chemo treatment, but each month I arrive not knowing what I will find out. Maybe things will have improved, but they might have deteriorated.

Maybe this disease spreads, too?

If so, how and to where?

Would I notice?

Would anyone notice?

Does a simple blood test reveal that?

I have no way of knowing other than my internal sense that things are going well. This cancer thing shines a light on my, and our, human frailty and vulnerability.

How has this changed my life? Well, firstly, I must hold in tension that I am anxious about whether this thing is retreating or still hanging around, and the fact that I am feeling well. Most of us go through our lives not fearing being told we have a bad thing going on inside us. Of course we do, or we would be living in a permanent state of fear. I don't want to live in such a state even now. And for the most part, I am not.

Often, I forget that I have this thing altogether and it's only the morning routine of taking one of the tablets (very expensive tablets at that) that are keeping me alive that reminds me.

I ask Dr Al whether we know if this disease has gone from me and should we do another bone marrow biopsy to check.

"Why bother?" he says.

"Well, personally, I can think of many reasons."

"We may find a tiny bit of evidence or nothing at all. But it doesn't mean that it has been eradicated. We can't be certain just yet. Maybe never."

"Oh."

"But you look really well, and you certainly don't look like a 62-year-old man."

"Thanks."

"And your blood numbers are all normal. Your haemoglobin is 132, WBC, platelets, U + Es and LFTs are all normal."

I'm glad. That's good.

Of course, I have no idea what these letters really mean other than that my red blood cells and white blood cells are behaving themselves and that my kidneys are functioning properly.

As the dead bad cells must vacate my body through my wee, it's important that my kidneys and liver can handle these without themselves becoming damaged. Also, I do not have excessive amounts of proteins in my blood, which is good, apparently.

Considering a year ago, when the state of the infection of my bone marrow was 95%, this is, according to Dr Al, one of the most impressive responses he has seen. I wish I could say that I had something to do with that, and maybe I have had. On the homeward journey, I reflect that the combination of brilliant science and faith has given me renewal. And I am humbled and thankful.

Has this thing changed my life? This is an odd thought. No, and yes.

I have not been forced to stop smoking (because I don't) or, eating the wrong things or drinking heavily (because I don't). I will have to get back to doing more physical exercise, but I am hampered still, firstly by weak back muscles that leave me with a sore back if I stand for too long or if I walk too far, and secondly by increasingly bad knees that will need replacing at some point in the not-too-distant future.

I have stopped air travel for now because of the pandemic. My business clients no longer require me to be in the USA or Asia or mainland Europe and we have not been able to take any overseas holidays.

I do wonder, of course, whether this travel contributed to the arrival of the disease. Who can say? My gut instinct says that, although at the time I thought nothing of spending hour upon hour in an airtight box with hundreds of other people, it cannot be healthy, and it could well have started the process and discombobulated my plot-forgetting cells. I am reflecting on these pressures we put on our bodies through our extraordinary lifestyles.

So, have I changed much? I am still a person who dreams big and, thus, I am constantly exploring how to improve the café's impact and how to find ways to change the world for good through my interactions with the hundreds of people I meet each year. I suspect this is not going to change as it is who I am; whether I have another five, 10 or 20 years to do this, only God knows.

As I write this, I am back on the road a bit, albeit in the UK only, and doing what I am best at – communicating challenging behaviours, and inspiring change and belief in the possible.

And I am feeling my age, which I am in denial about.

Pathetic, isn't it?

In some aspects of my life, I have become softer. One of my colleagues reckons that I have become softer overall and seem to view aspects of life with a softer heart and perspective. I like this thought, and I can feel it, by and large. However, in other aspects of my life, I feel I have become tetchier and more irritable. I am not sure how to explain this, other than when I was firstly ill and then totally brought down physically, I would oscillate between gratefulness and anger, between acceptance of kindness and intolerance and impatience. I suspect that such serious illness highlights our emotional immaturity and forces us to confront our mortal transience. Is it life-threatening or not?

I suspect many of us treat these things rather glibly until they touch us. For thousands of people, this has been their reality for the past two years as Covid-19 has struck without fear or favour throughout our societies. No one initially appreciated the extent of the life-threatening nature of Covid-19 and its ravages have left some confused, some bitter, some heartbroken, some utterly devastated, and some relieved. A full spectrum of human reactions and responses.

I believe that it has changed my life insofar as I am more acutely aware of my emotional extremes – extremes of fear and anxiety alongside hope, love and joy. And it is this that I often dwell upon. Our human existence is rawness itself. It is our responses to the normal, the mundane and the unpredicted, the unfathomable, the mysterious, that shape us. These do not define us, but they do reveal us. And I am ashamed to say that at times, I have been revealed to be seriously all over the place – protesting, sobbing, demanding, moody, as well as random moments of generosity, kindness, and uncontrollable laughing. I wonder if one way that this thing has changed my life is that I have felt the intensity of life in an undiluted way.

And I am still alive.

We hear stories of people who face near-death experiences and survive or recover from dreadful diagnoses, and then speak of having been given a second chance and wanting to do something more valuable with their lives. This is laudable and I do not want to denigrate it in any way. But, for me, I cannot say this is true. I do not feel I have been given a second chance because I don't feel I wasted or spent the first one yet. But, of course, this thing has impacted me profoundly.

As I have mentioned, I was constantly on the go and this past year has forced me to stop and slow. A bit.

Well, initially, a lot, as I was brought to a complete standstill. It was immensely frustrating.

This is the root of the mood swings, I suspect. Once fit, capable and with loads of energy, I am now not fit, and I must stand by as my sons do the DIY in my house for me, mainly the heavy lifting bits, you understand.

How naïve to think that this wouldn't impact me. Am I so superhuman? Preposterous!

My father went through the same thing.

I watched it. As he got older, he became less capable and didn't really admit this until the very last couple of years of his life. He died when he was 84. He hated it. It was an afront to his identity, his worth as a man, as a husband, as a human being. At times, I thought he was just plain obstinate, but I now know something of his sense of impending loss.

Bless him, though. He was still driving as a volunteer for the local community right up to the point where he could no longer do it in his 80th year. Not that I would have ever got in a car with him driving at this stage in his life.

I want to stay kind.

I want to stay warm-hearted.

At the monthly visit to the cancer clinic for my blood test last week, I met a man whom I had parked next to. As he struggled to open the door to his car (cars are so much wider these days), we said hello. His opening question is both direct and understandable. Thereafter, the conversation is surreal and, at the same time, profoundly human.

"What have you been in for today?" he asks.

"My monthly blood test, and you?"

"Similar, a monthly visit. What have you got?"

"Mine is non-Hodgkin's lymphoma – Waldenström macroglobulinemia. And you?"

"Blood too – multiple myeloma."

At this point, I am not sure how to respond. My brother-in-law has this cancer and is now, we fear, on the final downhill slope. We visited him very recently for the first time since the pandemic began and were shocked to discover that he is now confined to a bed in his front room and being cared for 24/7 by Caroline's sister and other carers. He is understandably depressed and the whole mood of the visit was rather difficult, given that I am feeling good. Myeloma is a killer, usually incurable. He has had it for about 10 years and has become more and more immobile.

Rafts of chemotherapy and treatments have prolonged his life, I am sure, but the quality of his life is rubbish. Everyone can see that. His only reason for hope or joy is his new granddaughters, both about 18 months old.

He won't see them make three, we suspect.

How should I engage with this stranger, then?

"Oh, golly, that's tough," I say.

He proceeds to tell me about being diagnosed just at the start of the pandemic and being brought down to earth with a complete halt when his doctor – none other than Dr. Al himself – told him the seriousness of his illness and forbade him from going skiing. He's had one bone marrow transplant and is on a cocktail of chemo and drugs.

He looks well, though. He is 58 and, rather like me, is a man who lived a full life. Like me, he was out of breath. Now, he has a blood disease that is going to eat at his bones and, in current probability, give him a maximum of 10 years. He is very chirpy.

That could have been me. It seems that my plasma cells produce subtly different para proteins that can be treated differently and managed, whereas his are less helpful. It's a bit like the subtle difference between a key lime tart and a lemon tart. A little bit of lime makes all the difference. When we say farewell, I sit in my car for a few moments and weep.

I say profoundly human because this conversation is remarkably honest and, as we are both facing some kind of similar health traumas and the associated anxieties, we have common ground upon which we share to empathise and sympathise. In my mind, this is one of the ways in which we are more similar than different as human beings. Just as we all rejoice at the birth of a new child or the fulfillment of a dream, we come together over suffering and anxiety.

The pandemic has re-taught us this and, for me, I have been

reminded that my life is a gift from God (in my case, I believe this) and that each day is an opportunity for wonder, for learning, for kindness, for joy and for pain.

For discovery and for revelation.

For love and for fearfulness.

This past year, for many of us, has been about breath. For me, it's been about breath and blood. I guess that's life in a nutshell. And for me, for now at least, I am grateful that where there should be blood and oxygen, there is some and it is cleaner and healthier and flowing in my veins.

Thank you, God.

Acknowledgment

This work would not have been possible without the encouragement from my wife of over forty years, Caroline, who laughed a lot through the drafts and whose calmness and resilience have helped me survive.

Thanks also to my kids for their continued belief in me and for sharing the nonsense of many episodes of this story.

A special thanks to my work colleagues and friends, far too many to mention by name, who stood by me when things looked bleak and continued asking me how I was doing. You know who you are and you have a special place in my heart.

It's odd to make a special mention to a dog, but my beloved golden retriever Mumford was a comfort in difficult times for me as he knew when to come close and reassure with his simple presence and warm hearted affection. I will miss him hugely.

I must also acknowledge the amazingly devoted and skilled staff in the NHS and all those people who continue to strive for cures for cancer of all types. You are angels in disguise.

Finally, my friend Jon Burr for his design for the cover and the folks at Amazon and Caroline for helping me edit this work and bring it to life.

www.ingramcontent.com/pod-product-compliance
Lightning Source LLC
Chambersburg PA
CBHW051213120626
46547CB00013B/1340